The COMPANIONS *in Christ*™
Network
www.companionsinchrist.org

So much more!

Companions in Christ is *so much more* than printed resources. It offers an ongoing LEADERSHIP NETWORK that provides:

- Opportunities to connect with other small groups who are also journeying through the *Companions in Christ* series
- Insights and testimonies from other *Companions in Christ* participants
- An online discussion room where you can share or gather information
- Training opportunities that develop and deepen the leadership skills used in formational groups
- Helpful leadership tips and articles as well as updated lists of supplemental resources
- A staff available to consult with you to meet the needs of your small group

Just complete this card and drop it in the mail, and you can enjoy the many benefits available through the *Companions in Christ* NETWORK!

Name: _____

Address: _____

City/State/Zip: _____

Church: _____

Email: _____ Phone: _____

WOFPB

For information about dates and locations of *Companions in Christ* Leader Orientations (Basic One-Day Training) and Leader Trainings (Advance Three-Day Training) visit **www.companionsinchrist.org**

Tear off and use as bookmark.

COMPANIONS *in Christ*®
The Way of Forgiveness

Please include your return address:

_____

_____

_____

BUSINESS REPLY MAIL

FIRST-CLASS MAIL PERMIT NO. 1540 NASHVILLE TN

POSTAGE WILL BE PAID BY ADDRESSEE

UPPER ROOM MINISTRIES
PO BOX 340012
NASHVILLE, TN 37203-9540

COMPANIONS
in Christ

The Way of Forgiveness

A Small-Group Experience
in Spiritual Formation

PARTICIPANT'S BOOK

Marjorie J. Thompson

UPPER
ROOM BOOKS®
NASHVILLE

Cover design: Bruce Gore

Design and implementation: Lori Putnam

Cover art: Carter Bock

Cover art rendering: Marjorie J. Thompson

Interior art flap: Rembrandt's *Return of the Prodigal Son*, Hermitage Museum,
            St. Petersburg, Russia / SuperStock

Interior icon development: Michael C. McGuire, settingPace

First printing: 2002

Library of Congress Cataloging-in-Publication

Thompson, Marjorie J., 1953–
        Companions in Christ: the way of forgiveness / Marjorie J. Thompson.
                p. cm.
Includes bibliographical references.
        ISBN 0-8358-0980-3 (alk. paper)
        1. Forgiveness—Religious aspects—Christianity. 2. Forgiveness—Study and teaching. 3. Small groups—Religious aspects—Christianity—Study and teaching. 4. Church group work. I. Title.
BV4647 .F55 T46 2002
253' .7—dc21   2002002283

Printed in the United States of America

**For more information on *Companions in Christ*
call 800-972-0433 or visit www.companionsinchrist.org**

Contents

Acknowledgments

The original twenty-eight-week *Companions in Christ* resource grew from a vision long held by Stephen Bryant, editor/publisher of Upper Room Ministries, and given shape by Marjorie J. Thompson, director of the Pathways Center of Upper Room Ministries. The vision, which has now grown into the Companions in Christ series, was realized through the efforts of many people over many years. It is important, then, that we acknowledge not just those individuals who were instrumental in the development of *Companions in Christ: The Way of Forgiveness*, but that we also express gratitude to those who envisioned and contributed to the foundational work, *Companions in Christ.*

Companions in Christ: The Way of Forgiveness

Companions in Christ: The Way of Forgiveness is the second title in a series of small-group resources rooted in the vision and design of *Companions in Christ*. The progression for the eight-week journey and the writing of the weekly articles in the Participant's Book for *Companions in Christ: The Way of Forgiveness* are the work of Marjorie J. Thompson. The daily exercises and the Leader's Guide are the shared work of Marjorie Thompson and Stephen Bryant in consultation with a staff advisory group that included Lynne Deming, Cindy

Helms, and Tony Peterson. An additional group made important contributions to *The Way of Forgiveness*, especially to the daily exercises in the Participant's Book and the "Deeper Explorations" in the Leader's Guide. This group was comprised of individuals who were experienced in spiritual formation or who took part in the development of the original resource, *Companions in Christ*. They provided valuable insight and theological guidance as well. This group included John Anderson, WG Henry, Wynn McGregor, John Penn, Flora Slosson Wuellner, and Carole Cotton Winn.

Companions in Christ

The core resource, *Companions in Christ*, was the result of a team of persons who shared a vision for creatively engaging persons in a journey of spiritual growth and discovery. The work of these people laid the foundation for each book in the Companions in Christ series. Janice T. Grana served as editor. The authors of the chapter articles were Gerrit Scott Dawson, Adele Gonzalez, E. Glenn Hinson, Rueben P. Job, Marjorie J. Thompson, and Wendy M. Wright. Stephen Bryant was the primary author of the daily exercises and the Leader's Guide. Marjorie Thompson created the original design and participated in the editing. Keith Beasley-Topliffe served as a consultant in the creation of the process for the small-group meetings and contributed numerous ideas that influenced the final shape of the resource. Members of advisory groups were Jeannette Bakke, Avery Brooke, Thomas Parker, Helen Pearson Smith, Luther E. Smith Jr., Eradio Valverde Jr., Diane Luton Blum, Carol Bumbalough, Ruth Torri, and Mark Wilson. Prior to publication, the following churches participated as test groups:

First United Methodist Church, Hartselle, Alabama
St. George's Episcopal Church, Nashville, Tennessee
Northwest Presbyterian Church, Atlanta, Georgia
Garfield Memorial United Methodist Church, Pepper Pike, Ohio
First United Methodist Church, Corpus Christi, Texas
Malibu United Methodist Church, Malibu, California

First United Methodist Church, Santa Monica, California
St. Paul United Methodist Church, San Antonio, Texas
Trinity Presbyterian Church, Arvada, Colorado
First United Methodist Church, Franklin, Tennessee
La Trinidad United Methodist Church, San Antonio, Texas
Aldersgate United Methodist Church, Slidell, Louisiana

Introduction

W elcome to *Companions in Christ: The Way of Forgiveness*, a small-group resource designed to help you explore Christ's call to live a forgiven and forgiving life. Over the course of eight weeks, you will explore the movement from guilt, shame, and anger to forgiveness and reconciliation. Jesus' understanding of the blessed life as expressed in his teachings from the Sermon on the Mount (Matthew 5–7) provides the larger context for this exploration. These teachings comprise some of the most profound and spiritually challenging ideas you could ever hope to realize in your life. It is a privilege to struggle with the challenge. Perhaps like Jacob wrestling with the angel (Gen. 32:22-32), you will emerge from the struggle with a blessing if you but ask!

This resource is the second title in a series, beginning with the twenty-eight week core resource in spiritual formation called *Companions in Christ*. Each successive title of Companions expands the core content in the same basic format.

The foundational resource, *Companions in Christ*, explored the Christian spiritual life under five headings: Journey, Scripture, Prayer, Call, and Spiritual Guidance. Each subsequent title in the Companions series will explore in greater depth some aspect of one of the four primary categories of spiritual practice already identified: scripture, prayer, vocation, and guidance.

The Way of Forgiveness falls under the heading of Christian vocation or call. Forgiveness and reconciliation, practices that give concrete expression to our calling as disciples of Jesus, say something profound about how we live out our faith in a world of daily realities far from ideal.

Few would claim it is an easy matter to learn to forgive those who have wounded us or to be reconciled to our enemies. The demands of Christian discipleship are challenging, to say the least. Jesus asks nothing short of complete conversion of life—a transformation of mind, heart, and action that reveals ever more fully the beauty and wholeness of his own life in us. This is what it means to be conformed to the image of Christ, the goal of spiritual formation in the Christian tradition. We cannot even consider this daunting prospect apart from the grace of God. Yet our theological heritage affirms that grace is already available to us in the person of Jesus Christ and is continually extended to us through the gift of the Holy Spirit. We gain access to grace most readily through faith, prayer, love for the deep truths of scripture, willingness to be guided by the Spirit, and offering ourselves in God's service.

Like the foundational *Companions in Christ,* this resource will help you deepen essential practices of the Christian life. The study focuses on your daily experience of God and your growing capacity to respond to grace with gratitude, trust, and love. Because this exploration occurs within a small group, you can expect increasingly to know the blessings of mutual support, encouragement, guidance, and accountability in Christian community. Your growth in faith and maturation in spirit will benefit your congregation also. Amid the various church conflicts and growing world tensions, our deepened capacity for forgiveness and reconciliation is more vital than ever.

About the Resource and Process

Like all Companions in Christ resources, *The Way of Forgiveness* has two primary components: individual reading and daily exercises throughout the week with this Participant's Book, and a weekly two-hour meeting based on suggestions in the Leader's Guide.

Each weekly chapter in the Participant's Book introduces new material and provides five daily exercises to help you reflect on your life in light of the chapter content. After the Preparatory Meeting of your group, you will begin a weekly cycle as follows: On day 1 you will be asked to read the chapter; on days 2–6 you will complete each of the five daily exercises (found at the end of each chapter). On day 7 you will meet with your group.

The daily exercises aim to help you move from information (knowledge about) to experience (knowledge of). An important part of this process is keeping a personal notebook or journal where you record reflections, prayers, and questions for later review and for reference at the weekly group meeting. The time commitment for one daily exercise is approximately thirty minutes.

Weekly meetings include time for sharing reflections on the exercises of the past week and for moving deeper into the content of the chapter through various learning and prayer experiences. Meetings begin and end with simple worship times and may include consideration of ways to share the group's discoveries with the congregation. You will need to bring your Participant's Book, your Bible, and your personal notebook or journal to each weekly group meeting.

An annotated resource list on pages 103–108 describes additional Upper Room book titles related to the theme of forgiveness.

The Companions in Christ Network

An additional dimension of resources in the *Companions in Christ* series is the Network. While you and your group are experiencing *Companions*, groups in other congregations will also be meeting. The Network provides opportunities for you to share your experiences with one another and to link in a variety of meaningful ways. As you move through the resource, upon occasion you will be invited to pray for another group's members, send greetings or encouragement, or receive their support for your group. Connecting in these ways will enrich your group's experience and the experience of those to whom you reach out. It will help you become aware of the wider reality of our companionship in the body of Christ across geographic and denominational lines.

The Network also provides a place to share conversation and information. The *Companions* Web site, www.companionsinchrist.org, has a discussion room where you can offer insights, voice questions, and respond to others in an ongoing process of shared learning. The site lists other *Way of Forgiveness* groups and their geographical locations so that you can make connections as you feel led.

The *Companions* Network is a versatile and dynamic component of the larger *Companions* resource. The Network toll-free number is 800-972-0433.

Your Personal Notebook or Journal

Keeping a journal or personal notebook (commonly called journaling) will be one of the most important dimensions of your experience with *Companions in Christ: The Way of Forgiveness*. The Participant's Book gives you daily spiritual exercises each week. More often than not, you will be asked to note your thoughts, reflections, questions, feelings, or prayers in relation to the exercises.

Even if you are totally inexperienced in this kind of personal writing, you may find that it becomes second nature quickly. Your thoughts may start to pour out of you, giving expression to an inner life that has never been released. If, on the other hand, you find the writing difficult or cumbersome, give yourself permission to try it in a new way. Because a journal is "for your eyes only," you may choose any style that suits you. You need not worry about making your words sound beautiful or about writing with good grammar and spelling. You don't even need to write complete sentences! Jotting down key ideas, insights, or musings is just fine. You might want to doodle while you think or sketch an image that comes to you. Make journaling fun and relaxed. No one will see what you write, and you have complete freedom to share with the group only what you choose of your reflections.

There are two important reasons for keeping a journal or personal notebook as you move through *The Way of Forgiveness*. First, the process of writing thoughts down clarifies them. They become more specific and concrete. Sometimes we really do not know what we think until we see our thoughts on paper, and often the process of writing itself generates new creative insight. Second, this personal record captures what you experience inwardly over time, helping you track changes in your thinking and growth of insight. People's memories are notoriously fragile and fleeting in this regard. Specific feelings or creative connections you may have had two weeks ago, or even three days ago, are hard to recall without a written record. Even though your journal cannot capture all that goes through your mind in a single reflection period, it will serve as a reminder that you will draw on during small-group meetings each week.

Begin by purchasing a book that you can use for this purpose. It can be as simple as a spiral-bound notebook or as fancy as a clothbound blank book. Some people prefer lined paper and some unlined. You will want, at minimum, something more permanent than a ring-binder or paper pad. The Upper Room has made available a companion journal for this resource that you can purchase if you so desire.

When you begin the daily exercises, have your journal and pen or pencil at hand. You need not wait until you have finished reading and thinking an exercise through completely. Learn to stop and write as you go. Think on paper. Feel free to write anything that comes to you, even if it seems to be "off the topic." It may turn out to be more relevant or useful than you first think. If the process seems clumsy at first, don't fret. Like any spiritual practice, it gets easier over time, and its value becomes more apparent.

Here is how your weekly practice of journaling is shaped. On the first day after your group meeting, read the new chapter. Jot down your responses to the reading: "aha" moments, questions, points of disagreement, images, or any other reflections you wish to record. You may prefer to note these in the margins of the chapter. Over the next five days, you will do the exercises for the week, recording either general or specific responses as they are invited. On the day of the group meeting, it will be helpful to review what you have written through the week, perhaps marking portions you would like to share in the group. Bring your journal with you to meetings so that you can refer to it directly or refresh your memory of significant moments you want to paraphrase during discussion times. With time, you may find that journaling helps you to think out your own pattern of living and that you will be able to see more clearly how God is at work in your life.

Your Group Meeting

The weekly group meeting is divided into four segments. First you will gather for a brief time of worship and prayer. This offers an opportunity to set aside the many concerns of the day and center on God's presence and guidance as you begin your group session.

The second section of the meeting is called "Sharing Insights." During this time you will be invited to talk about your experiences with the daily exercises. The group leader will participate as a member and share his or her responses as well. Generally the sharing by each member will be brief and related to specific exercises. This is an important time for your group to learn and practice what it means to be a community of persons seeking to listen to God and to live more faithfully as disciples of Christ. The group provides a supportive space to explore your listening, your spiritual practices, and how you are attempting to integrate those practices into daily life. Group members need not comment or offer advice to one another. Rather the group members help you, by their attentiveness and prayer, to pay attention to what has been happening in your particular response to the daily exercises. The group does not function as a traditional support group that offers suggestions or help to one another. Rather the group members trust that the Holy Spirit is the guide and that they are called to help one another listen to that guidance.

The "Sharing Insights" time presents a unique opportunity to learn how God works differently in each of our lives. Our journeys, while varied, are enriched by others' experiences. We can hold one another in prayer, and we can honor each other's experience. Through this part of the meeting, you will see in fresh ways how God's activity may touch or address our lives in unexpected ways. The group will need to establish some ground rules to facilitate the sharing. For example, you may want to be clear that each person speak only about his or her own beliefs, feelings, and responses and that all group members have permission to share only what and when they are ready to share. Above all, the group needs to maintain confidentiality so that what is shared in the group stays in the group. This part of the group meeting will be much less meaningful if persons interrupt and try to comment on what is said or try to "fix" what they see as a problem. The leader will close this part of the meeting by calling attention to any patterns or themes that seem to emerge from the group's sharing. These patterns may point to a word that God is offering to the group. Notice that the group leader functions both as a participant and as someone who aids the process by listening and summarizing the key insights that have surfaced.

The third segment of the group meeting is called "Deeper Explorations." This part of the meeting may expand on ideas contained in the week's chapter, offer practice in the spiritual disciplines introduced in the chapter or exercises, or give group members a chance to reflect on the implications of what they are learning for themselves and for their church. It offers a common learning experience for the group and a chance to go deeper in our understanding of how we can share more fully in the mind, heart, and work of Jesus Christ.

As it began, the group meeting ends with a brief time of worship, an ideal time for the group to share special requests for intercession that might come from the conversation and experience of the meeting or other prayer requests that arise naturally from the group.

Limits and Responsibilities of the Companions in Christ: The Way of Forgiveness *Group*

If you are a person who is experiencing or inflicting abuse or if you are aware of abuse that is occurring, contact the National Domestic Violence Hotline at 1-800-799-7233 for assistance. *Companions in Christ* groups, while caring and discerning, are not intended or trained to respond to these issues.

You should know that while most *Companions in Christ* groups agree to hold in confidence information that is shared by the members, such sharing is not legally recognized as "privileged communication" and is not protected by law.

Invitation to the Journey

The weeks that you give to *The Way of Forgiveness* offer a unique opportunity to focus on your relationship with Jesus Christ and to grow in your response to God's presence and guidance. Other members of your small group, truly your companions on the journey, will encourage your searching and learning as you encourage theirs.

We invite you now to open yourself inwardly to the grace that will be given during this exploration of our call to forgive and be reconciled with others, even as we have been forgiven by and reconciled to God in Jesus Christ. Claim boldly from God whatever you feel you need in order to approach this topic. Few other practices can bring us so close to the mind and heart of Christ as these blessed attitudes and actions. May the grace of the Holy Spirit enfold and uphold you.

Week 1

Living in God's Blessing

*D*o you have any idea of who you really are? I suspect that if you asked your family members, friends, and coworkers who they are, you would get as many answers as persons. We tend to think that we are the sum of our family connections, accomplishments, interests, and line of work. Consistently we introduce ourselves in such terms: I am the son or daughter of so and so; I am married and have so many children (or grandchildren); I am an architect, musician, homemaker, or software engineer. I am an avid reader, fly fisher, sports fan, or traveler.

We do not think of ourselves primarily as human beings who bear the imprint of divine life in our very souls. Few persons would introduce themselves by saying, "I am a child of God like you." We focus on those factors that make our lives seem distinctive, if not distinguished. In this way we attempt to secure our sense of identity. Yet our identity will always feel insecure if it is rooted primarily in external realities such as our achievements or connections. Such sources of identity are of limited value in themselves and, by nature, highly changeable.

Teresa of Avila, a sixteenth-century saint, had an astonishing sense of what the human soul truly is. In her most profound work, *Interior Castle*, she writes, "I don't find anything comparable to the magnificent

In order to receive and offer reconciliation, we need to be able to claim a self whose very identity lies in God, a self which we know can neither be given away nor stolen.

—Roberta C. Bondi

beauty of a soul and its marvelous capacity. Indeed, our intellects, however keen, can hardly comprehend it, just as they cannot comprehend God; but [the Creator] says that [we were] created…in [God's] own image and likeness." She goes on to say, "We know we have souls. But we seldom consider the precious things that can be found in this soul, or who dwells within it, or its high value. Consequently, little effort is made to preserve its beauty."[1] God created us for a purpose more astonishing and sublime than we can imagine. Every great Christian theologian and saint has borne witness to this high purpose. The human being is created in the divine image and likeness in order to have continual and intimate communion with the One who made us. We are created to love and be loved by God, born to serve and be served by Christ, destined to enjoy the vitality of the Holy Spirit and in turn receive God's delight in us forever! Such is God's good pleasure and our highest bliss.

In the midst of ordinary life, however, it is hard to remember these things. Clearly we have yet to fulfill our highest purpose. What should be native to our hearts is either a blurred myth of an original state of innocence (the garden of Eden) or a dim vision of future sanctification and heavenly joy (the banquet of the kingdom). We are caught between veils, so to speak—the veil that shrouds our original glory and the veil that clouds our perception of a promised paradise. We live in a certain dimness of soul, yearning and hoping for the transformation that would make of this world the very kingdom of God. While beauty and goodness can be found between the veils, the world we know is certainly far from the divine reign. It is full of pain, alienation, hostility, and suspicion. It is a place of disaster and disease, of ignorance and illusion, of unmet needs and betrayed trust.

Yet this is precisely why the gospel is such good news. Into our darkness a great light has come! "The true light, which enlightens everyone" (John 1:9) has come to us from the very realm of God and with the very power of God (vv. 1-5). This light came to reveal to us who we truly are and how we are meant to live: "To all who received him…he gave power to become children of God" (v. 12). Christ came to restore to us our original heritage as sons and daughters of the

As St. Augustine declared, our hearts are restless until they find their rest in God.…We have a God-hunger which only God can satisfy.

—Desmond M. Tutu

living God. Indeed, scripture tells us that he himself "is the image of the invisible God" (Col. 1:15), pure and unalloyed. He reveals, models, and offers to us what he himself is.

Jesus embodies the new life we are called to live in faith and faithfulness. This new life is also very concisely taught by him. Nowhere in the Gospels is the new life given more powerful expression than in those teachings that have come to be called the "Sermon on the Mount." This portion of Matthew's Gospel covers three full chapters (5–7), but we will focus on the fifth chapter for this week's reflection.

The utterly transformed perspective of the Christ-life is shockingly forceful in Matthew 5. It begins with the Beatitudes (vv. 1-11) where Jesus extols the blessedness of virtually every human state or experience we would typically prefer to avoid. Take a moment to read through these verses and see if you agree with this perception. Neediness, grief, meekness, mercy, a willingness to be persecuted—such states are widely regarded as painful, weak, or too pure for human reality. These verses immediately challenge our standard definitions of what it means to be "blessed." Jesus doesn't have a thing to say here about material blessing, for example, or security.

A number of distinct teachings follow the Beatitudes. Most of the teachings begin with the formula: "You have heard that it was said....But I say to you...." With these words Jesus calls his followers to a higher standard of goodness, a deeper life of godliness, than that held up by the conventional religious leaders of his time. He seems determined that God's children understand the spiritual roots of God's law and not be satisfied with mere legalism. Every law contains an inward depth; higher principles of humility, simplicity, mercy, and love reveal the perfection of God's life in us.

When Jesus calls us to "be perfect, therefore, as your heavenly Father is perfect" (v. 48), he clearly does *not* mean a pinched, legalistic concept of perfection—the very thing he has been warning against in each instance! He points rather to a deep, God-designed wholeness in the human spirit. Such wholeness is not the result of taking a deep breath, gritting our teeth, and willing it to be so. We cannot make ourselves perfect by our own efforts. Wholeness is a gift that comes

to us gradually through the process of daily living with God. Jesus tells us to abide in him as he abides in us (John 15:4). As we learn what it means to dwell consciously, moment by moment, in the divine presence, God graciously shares with us the gift of Christ's own wholeness. Such perfection embodies the fullness of human life as God intended it, reflecting the divine image and likeness with rich and sparkling clarity.

Scan the rest of Matthew 5. These various teachings tell us a great deal about what the image of God looks like in daily life. In a life shaped by grace and guided by the Spirit, we become salt and light in this world. Perhaps we bring the savor of gentle strength and simplicity to a commercialized world of monied power; perhaps we offer the generous flavors of God's love to the flat, tasteless depression of persons imprisoned in self-loathing. And what else?

In a life fed by the inner springs of divine love, we can go beyond the external demands of God's law to its very heart. In this realm, we do not act from anger against others; we quickly reconcile ourselves to sisters and brothers with whom we have been in conflict; we speak our truth without exaggeration or distortion; out of sheer generosity of heart, we offer more to others than they can rightly claim; we love those who hate us and pray for those who misuse us. By grace we can live by a higher law than retribution, guided by spiritual principles that transcend common notions of human justice. And in all this, our experience does not resemble victimhood, but rather joyous freedom! Jesus has thoroughly and permanently redefined blessedness.

Yet to the eyes of the world and to the worldliness within us, Jesus' teachings on the blessed life sound like absurd idealism, impossibility, pure folly. To live this way resembles anything but freedom. Indeed, it looks more like serious psychological weakness and the dangerous acceptance of abuse. Few things are more difficult for us than to comprehend and live the freedom of God's beloved children.

It takes great willingness and a lot of practice to begin to see life from God's perspective. We need the guidance of scripture, prayer, and one another in the process. For that very reason we will be delving into

These words do not summon us to weak submission and powerlessness but to a different kind of power. This new power neither invades nor defends, yet it is the toughest, most enduring and transforming energy in the world—an empowered vulnerability that is not victimhood.

—Flora Slosson Wuellner

the kind of life that takes Jesus' teachings in Matthew 5 seriously. We will also thoughtfully consider Teresa of Avila's plea that we make a genuine effort to value and preserve the beauty of our souls.

In particular, we will explore the rich ore of forgiveness and reconciliation in the gold mine of biblical faith. This precious ore is not easily mined, for it is embedded in the hard rock of our fears, hurts, angers, and hatreds. But we have the best of all possible guides, the Holy Spirit, whom we often hear in the voices and stories of fellow believers as well as in the pages of holy writ.

These weeks may represent for you a fresh start in exploring forgiveness and reconciliation. Or they may help you continue and deepen work already stirring, by God's grace, in your heart. Dealing with issues of forgiveness and reconciliation is a continual journey for all of us and will remain so as long as we live in a world where sin and death seem to prevail so triumphantly. It is a journey well worth the struggle, nonetheless, for it takes us on a path of increasing freedom, release, and joy. May we discover for ourselves why the conditions set forth by Jesus in the Sermon on the Mount are indeed sources of life and blessing!

DAILY EXERCISES

The way of forgiveness begins with an awareness of the extraordinary quality of life for which God creates us and continues to invite us to practice. The focus of your daily exercises this first week is "the magnificent beauty of a soul and its marvelous capacity" (see pages 17–18) as reflected in the fifth chapter of the Gospel of Matthew.

Be sure to read Week 1, "Living in God's Blessing," before you begin these exercises. Keep your journal or notebook beside you to record your thoughts, questions, prayers, or images. In preparation for each exercise, take a few moments to quiet yourself and place the concerns of the day in God's hands. Open your heart to the guidance of the Holy Spirit.

EXERCISE 1

Read Mark 1:9-11. In his book *Mending the Heart*, John Claypool writes, "What Jesus heard when coming up from the waters of baptism is exactly what God wants to communicate to every single soul."[2] Ponder the meaning of each phrase of Jesus' baptismal blessing. Overhear it as a truth Jesus wants to share with you: You are God's beloved. Translate the blessing into your own words as it applies to your identity in God.

Memorize the blessing and make it part of your life. Try tying it to your breathing in and out in small phrases that feel comfortable (for example, "You are my child, the beloved / with you I am well pleased"). Spend some time soaking in the unconditional love that God bestows upon you. Then take this blessing with you through the day and also see others—your children, a parent, a person on the street— through the transfiguring lens of the blessing.

EXERCISE 2

Read Genesis 12:1-3. God's promise to Abraham, "I will bless you…so that you will be a blessing," reflects God's gift and call to all people of faith. In your journal list three people and three circumstances through which God has blessed you with an appreciation of "the magnificent beauty of [your] soul and its marvelous capacity." What gift did each person or situation give you? Now reflect on specific people and circumstances that God has blessed through you. List them also. What gift do you hope others received through you?

EXERCISE 3

Read Psalm 136. Expand this psalm of thanksgiving by adding to it particular signs of God's love in your life. Continue what you began yesterday, listing additional people and circumstances through which God has loved and molded you for the better and that God has loved and molded through you. Observe which list is longer and what that may say. Then, following the form of Psalm 136, transform your list into a litany of thanksgiving for the steadfast love of God in your life. For example:

> O give thanks to the God of gods…who gave me life through the love of Joe and Mabel, for God's steadfast love endures forever; who opened my eyes through family tragedy to the pain of others, for God's steadfast love endures forever.

Slowly pray your litany aloud, savoring each memory and thanking God.

EXERCISE 4

Read Matthew 5:1-11. Explore what the author means when she writes (on page 19) that in the Beatitudes Jesus challenges "our standard definitions of what it means to be 'blessed.'" On one side of your page, list the kinds of blessings most people (including you) generally wish for. On the other side, list key words from Jesus' descriptions of blessing. How would you characterize the difference?

Make a note of the times in your life when you felt closest to God or when your depth of soul was enriched and proven in a special way. Recall whether at the time the experiences were positive or negative, welcome or unwelcome. Turn each of those gifted times into a personal beatitude. For example, "Blessed was I during my walk through

the dark valley, for it humbled me and taught me God's faithful presence." "Blessed am I in my ongoing recovery, for I am regaining my freedom and becoming more the person God created me to be." "Blessed were we when we participated in a homeless ministry, for we found a larger purpose than our own life together."

EXERCISE 5

Read Matthew 5:13. In *The Message*, Eugene Peterson paraphrases this verse: "Let me tell you why you are here. You're here to be salt-seasoning that brings out the God-flavors of this earth. If you lose your saltiness, how will people taste godliness?"

Reflect on ways that people experienced Jesus' life as such salt-seasoning. Consider how Jesus' followers may have experienced his saltiness in contrast to his detractors. Who adds the salt-seasoning that brings out the "God-flavors" of your life? For whom are you this kind of salt-seasoning? Record your thoughts in your journal.

Remember to review the insights recorded in your notebook or journal for the week in preparation for the group meeting.

Week 2
Releasing Shame and Guilt

*J*esus makes it clear that key characteristics mark the life of blessedness. Those who know their need of God are blessed; those who are sorrowful, gentle of spirit, and full of mercy are blessed; those who yearn above all for righteousness, whose hearts are pure, who suffer persecution for the cause of right are blessed; those who are willing continually to make peace are blessed.

These are hard lessons for us to hear, much less to learn. Our notions of being blessed typically lean toward an abundance of food, family love, good education, work opportunities, pleasant surroundings, and physical security. We crave and strive for these blessings in our lives. We may feel that our way of life is threatened when they are in short supply, and we are willing to fight aggressively to secure them since we have come to think of them as inalienable human rights.

All these things are indeed blessings. But they are not, it seems, the essence of the God-blessed life. In his usual fashion, Jesus invites us to consider deeper and more abiding matters of the heart. He directs us to the temper of our souls. And he does so because we are God's beloved children as he is God's beloved Son. He wants us to know and live from this deep truth. Jesus has the long view of eternity in mind in all that he teaches. Time, a remarkable gift, becomes a medium for learning how to live as God's beloved. But we find it

We do not expect to hear ourselves called the Beloved.
—Henri J. M. Nouwen

difficult to live this blessed life, in part because of the world's strong draw upon us. From our particular point and place in history, we live within the bounds of what we experience, observe, and believe.

Life experiences and choices, with their train of feelings and reactions, can lead us far from the knowledge of our soul-deep identity. The two primary emotional states with power to rob us of this soul memory are shame and guilt. What we do with shame and guilt are critical keys in our ability to handle forgiveness and reconciliation. But we need first to understand each one and distinguish between them. Basically shame has to do with our feelings about who we are, while guilt is related to our feelings about what we do.

One is guilty for what one did or did not do. One is ashamed of who one is.

—William Moremen

We may feel tremendous shame about who we are because of addictive behaviors, dysfunctional patterns, or dark secrets in our family life. We may feel shame due to consistent negative messages we received and believed about ourselves from parents, siblings, or teachers: "You are a bad girl or boy." "You are always so clumsy; why can't you be more careful?" "What a stupid child you are; you'll never amount to anything." Equally devastating are cultural messages of shame. Society has many ways to tell us that we are somehow less than fully acceptable because of such things as our gender, our skin color, our mental or physical capacities, or even the shape of our bodies. Such messages can make us feel permanently inadequate or innately inferior. As if we were damaged goods worth only a discount rate, we may habitually devalue ourselves and our abilities.

Another source of shame for many people comes from certain strains of our religious culture. Most of us have encountered in one guise or another a shaming brand of Western Christianity. The impact of this theology is described with uncomfortable poignancy by Roberta Bondi in her autobiographical writings. Examining an adult life "full of vague guilt," she realizes that her childhood experience of revivalist religion in rural Kentucky instilled in her an early awareness "that there was something fatally wrong with me."[1] For example, the ethos of her family and faith communicated that she was irretrievably guilty for being female, a daughter of the original sinner Eve. "Under the circumstances," she writes, "the language of sin gave me a way to explain myself to myself. It told me what was wrong with me, why I felt as though I stood perpetually under the judgment of the whole universe. As a child, the meaning of 'sin' was relatively straightforward. My very being was so sinful that God himself was enraged."[2] This sense of *intrinsic* unworthiness is the crux of shame, a truth Bondi recognizes later as an adult after trying vainly to repent her way out of what she had thought was guilt: "I did not need to repent. I needed to be rescued from my shame. And this is what I now could see was exactly what Jesus as the privileged son of God, as God's own self, had chosen to do by casting in his lot with not only me but with all women and men the world would shame and reduce to nothing for simply being who they are."[3]

Bondi's story helps us to see that forgiveness does not apply to shame in itself. If shame is purely related to who we are, in matters we have no choice about (gender, skin color, a limiting physical condition, poverty, and so forth), forgiveness has no meaning. What we need in such cases is the healing of self-worth, not forgiveness. But wherever shame is linked to genuine guilt, forgiveness regains a critical role in the healing process.

We may see the connection between shame and guilt in situations where shame wears a public face. When we are caught doing something wrong or something considered shameful in our culture, we must endure the humiliation of being known as someone who would do such a thing. This is often called "losing face," a telling expression. When we lose face we lose our cultivated pose, the public image we wish to show to the world. Often our faces literally burn with embarrassment as we feel the eyes of others judging us.

Jim, a friend of mine, remembers vividly an incident that generated this kind of shame. He was nine years old. Jim had always admired the penknife at the small grocery store in his town. Each time he and his father shopped, Jim was irresistibly drawn to the shelf that held the knife. One day following a shopping trip, Jim's dad discovered the knife tucked neatly into Jim's pocket. His dad knew immediately what had happened, and Jim's whole being burned with the shame and guilt of his act. His father required that he return the knife to the

store owner, admit his guilt, and offer an apology. Because the town had only the one store, Jim relived his guilt and shame for many years, each time he revisited the small store.

Some of us, due to our personal or cultural histories, are more prone to shame than others. But all of us at times know the burden of guilt. We feel guilt over things we have done—mistakes we have made, judgments that proved false, forgetting things in a way that hurt someone. We also feel guilt over things we have not done—failing to complete a necessary task, neglecting to write a lonely family member or friend, missing an opportunity to act when it could have made a difference. Guilt is both a subjective feeling (psychological reality) and an objective truth (spiritual reality). The feeling and the truth are not always identical. I may feel guilty for something that is not really my fault or for failing to meet unrealistic expectations I have set for myself that have little to do with God's intentions for me. Conversely, I may not feel guilty at all and may even be unaware of things for which I bear much responsibility. The spiritual reality of guilt resides in what God knows about our human failings and weaknesses, not necessarily what we know consciously. No doubt that is why the psalmist speaks of hidden faults and prays,

> Search me, O God, and know my heart;
> test me and know my thoughts.
> See if there is any wicked way in me,
> and lead me in the way everlasting.
> —Psalm 139:23-24

As we can see, the dynamics of guilt and shame are often closely linked. After all, what we do reflects for good or ill on who we are.

It is part of our fallen human condition to suffer shame and guilt in various ways. Sometimes our absorption in these feelings blinds us to any deeper reality. In her book *Dead Man Walking*, Sister Helen Prejean recounts her experiences as a spiritual advisor to two convicted murderers on death row, Patrick Sonnier and Robert Lee Willie. At a point of great emotional vulnerability Patrick admits, "I have never known real love."[4] The lack of felt love as a child had translated

No matter how guilty you feel..., no matter how guilty you may actually be, no matter how isolated you are,...Jesus Christ comes also to you.... He does not want to be without you.

—George Hunsinger

into an inability to care about others. Sister Helen's genuine concern for Pat helps him to experience love for the first time and, therefore, begin to see his own worth. When Sister Helen tells Robert Willie "that despite his crime, despite the terrible pain he has caused, he is a human being and he has a dignity that no one can take from him, that he is a son of God," Robert mumbles incredulously, "Ain't nobody ever called me no son of God before. I've been called a son-of-a-you-know-what lots of times but never no son of God."[5] Robert Willie probably had believed from an early age that he was "a son-of-a-you-know-what," and he was proving with his way of life that this was indeed his identity. Again Sister Helen's patient but unsentimental care helps Robert see another side of who he is. The possibility of a deeper human identity in God's love begins to emerge for him.

In a peculiar way, Robert Willie articulates a mind-set many Christian believers subtly share. Although our sins may seem minor compared to his, we may feel acutely conscious of our shortcomings and uncertain about how God's mercy will apply to us personally. Do we dare to believe that we really are beloved children of God, called into the glorious divine light to become the spiritually mature sons and daughters God created us to be? Do we dare believe forgiveness is possible? Perhaps we have known too much brokenness and pain to believe that we are truly destined in Christ to be like him. We may wonder if it is simply a wistful ideal to imagine that "when he is revealed, we will be like him, for we will see him as he is" (1 John 3:2); or that "He will transform the body of our humiliation that it may be conformed to the body of his glory, by the power that also enables him to make all things subject to himself" (Phil. 3:21).

Yet this is the great promise and hope of our faith: In Christ we become an entirely new creation! All that is old in us—the useless ideas, the faithless attitudes, the tightly held fears and destructive behaviors—will pass away as we give ourselves more fully to God. In their place will come gifts of the Spirit—new ways of understanding, believing, and acting that belong to the mind and heart of Jesus. All the Creator asks is that we be utterly honest before God, to open ourselves to grace, to abide in Christ our Redeemer, and to give ourselves

How is forgiveness possible? Forgiveness exists already— now and eternally. We do not create it; we enter it.
—Flora Slosson Wuellner

in love as much as we can each day. Only the Holy Spirit working in us can accomplish the new creation God intends each of us to be. We do not create the pattern of human holiness—it already exists and is shown to us in Christ. We do not make ourselves holy through great and diligent spiritual practice; only God can make us holy. We must be willing to change and open to the work of grace in us.

As we allow ourselves to be touched by grace, we discover more and more what true blessedness is. In the light of God's healing and forgiving love, our shame and guilt are gradually transformed into the virtues of humility and confident dependence on God. Jesus' words on the Mount concerning what it means to be blessed start to make sense. We find ourselves less tied up in the world's definitions of blessing and freer to participate in the life of blessedness Jesus describes. The Holy Spirit working within our hearts accomplishes this change. As the apostle Paul puts it,

> Now the Lord is the Spirit, and where the Spirit of the Lord is, there is freedom. And all of us, with unveiled faces, seeing the glory of the Lord as though reflected in a mirror, are being transformed into the same image from one degree of glory to another; for this comes from the Lord, the Spirit.
>
> —2 Corinthians 3:17-18

Part of the joy of our time together is discovering where the Spirit of the Lord will move us in our understanding and experience of God's blessing in relation to forgiveness. May our hearts be open!

People can be transformed. Perhaps you have been transformed in one way or another by God's goodness. Grant God the freedom to transform your enemy, too.
—L. William Countryman

DAILY EXERCISES

This week you will be reflecting on the nature of sin, our alienation from God that obscures our deepest and blessed soul identity. Experiences of guilt and shame and the memories with which they haunt us reveal clearly our need for grace and forgiveness. Read Week 2, "Releasing Shame and Guilt," before you begin these exercises. Keep your journal at hand to record reflections and questions. Remember to quiet yourself, release concerns to God, and open both mind and heart to the Spirit's work.

EXERCISE 1

Read Genesis 1:26-31. Take a five-minute walk to marvel at the wonder of God's creation, repeating some portion of this verse with every breath or step: "God saw everything…and indeed, it was very good." Find a place to sit. See the sights and listen to the sounds around you. Quietly pay attention to the evidence of your own fragile existence in your breathing and beating heart. Give thanks to God for the sheer gift and goodness of your life created in God's image and for the earth you share with other creatures.

As you affirm the goodness of God's creation, where do you also become aware of things around you that obscure God's blessing and depreciate the sacredness of human life? Record your experience and thoughts in your journal.

EXERCISE 2

Read Genesis 3:1-12. When Adam and Eve stop listening to their Maker and listen instead to the voice of temptation, they lose the sense of their blessed identity and feel shame. Yet in their hiding, God seeks them with the question, "Where are you?" Ponder this question and listen for God's searching call in your life. Take a moment to locate yourself before God. Write in your journal your response to the question.

Spend a few minutes in prayer, presenting yourself to God and saying, "Lord, here I am." Listen for God's response. During the day,

when you are tempted to hide behind a facade or fall into self-concern, remember God's calling out to you and respond, "Lord, here I am." Then trust and obey what you hear.

EXERCISE 3

Read Luke 15:11-24. (You may want to look again at the Rembrandt reproduction at the back of this book.) Revisit the depth of "lostness" in the prodigal son when "he began to be in need." Though still beloved in the heart of the father, he remained far from his true home. This son suffered a state of terrible indignity and shame for a Jew, having "hired himself out…to feed the pigs." Meditate on verses 14-17 and locate yourself imaginatively in the boy's place.

Ask the Lord to show you where you are wallowing in some past failure or misdeed, some form of shame or guilt. Reflect on the effects: missing the joy in life, feeling distant from God, or remaining alienated from certain persons. Then ask yourself, *What is keeping me from deciding to "get up and go" to a place of grace?* Ask God to help you answer this question. Record thoughts and insights in your journal.

EXERCISE 4

Read Matthew 26:14-16, 20-25, 47-50; 27:1-5. This is the tragic account of Judas's betrayal of Jesus and his hanging himself out of guilt. Imagine, had there been opportunity, what Jesus might have said to Judas when "he repented" (Matt. 27:3-4). What moral failure or guilt hangs heavily on you and cuts you off from peace with God? What painful memories of your actions bring suffering, and how do these memories and suffering affect your life? Write out the memory of a wrong for which you still carry guilt. Offer what you have written to Christ. Then write what you imagine Christ has desired to say and is saying to you. What is he inviting or challenging you to do?

EXERCISE 5

Read Psalm 25; 1 John 4:16-19. The psalmist answers his own request for deliverance from shame with the prayer, "Be mindful of your mercy, O LORD, and of your steadfast love." Sometimes we become trapped in shame or guilt because we are not mindful of God's mercy. We have not fully taken in the assurances of love that come from others and from God. What and who help you to know "and believe the love that God has for us" (1 John 4:16)? List several persons through whom you have experienced acceptance and love in ways that overcame shame and guilt. What assurances has God given you through them that you need to remember? Write a note of thanks to at least one of these persons and tell him or her about the gift he or she has given you.

Remember to review the insights recorded in your notebook or journal for the week in preparation for the group meeting.

Facing Our Anger

We are perhaps beginning to grasp just what this life of blessedness is that Jesus entices us to consider in his Sermon on the Mount. We know it represents a form of blessing not well understood by the world or by the worldliness within us. We may see that to live this way, as Jesus did, is to experience what it means to be beloved sons and daughters of God. The more we know our belovedness, the more freely we may live by the measure of Jesus' own example in the power of loving humility and transforming mercy. Here lie the spiritual roots of forgiveness and reconciliation. But the possibility of forgiveness and reconciliation can be as difficult to embrace as the notion of our belovedness.

One feeling that can effectively block our progress toward forgiveness is anger. Anger, a multifaceted reality, has both positive and negative sides. We tend to see the negative side more readily. Anger in others often generates fear in us. We can probably trace our fear back to the early years, when as children we found ourselves particularly vulnerable to the punishments that resulted from adult anger. Being punished probably stirred up feelings of anger in response, even if we knew we deserved it. Such reactive anger was stronger if we felt we had been punished unfairly, an experience no child has ever escaped! Yet our culture generally does not encourage children to express anger, and it often punishes immature expressions of this

emotion. No wonder we have learned to fear anger in ourselves as well as in others.

The destructive potential of anger affects us all. If we experienced a great deal of family dysfunction and adult anger while growing up, we probably have anxious associations with the feeling of anger. Those of us who were blessed with a relatively peaceful family life have still been exposed to violent expressions of anger dramatized and glorified in movies, videos, and popular music. News journalists carry reports on the most unsettled world situations where angry conflicts erupt in seemingly endless cycles. Politics too tends to thrive on anger, often drawing its most fervent support for policy platforms from the submerged rage of disaffected citizens.

Our immensely ambivalent relationship to anger stems from its strong association with negative power. We don't want to feel it; yet we do. Often it seems easier or safer simply to deny or suppress this emotion. There is much we need to understand about anger in order to recognize it fully, value what we can learn from it, and channel its destructive potential into constructive energy. Our view of this emotion and how we choose to use it is a deeply spiritual matter.

Biblical writers certainly acknowledged the reality of human anger and its effects. They also accepted a concept of divine wrath that expressed God's larger good purpose. On the whole, the Bible portrays human anger in itself as neither good nor bad. It is a morally neutral psychological fact but potentially dangerous. Cain's anger after the Lord accepts Abel's offering but not his prompts the Lord to say to Cain, "Why are you angry, and why has your countenance fallen?…Sin is lurking at the door; its desire is for you, but you must master it" (Gen. 4:6-7). The writer of Ephesians counsels, "Be angry but do not sin" (4:26*a*). Jesus himself becomes angry with various religious leaders and with money changers in the Temple. As Christians, we believe that Jesus lived a life of perfect obedience to God. Surely then anger, a natural human emotion, may have some benefit when properly directed but can become a devouring beast if we do not master it.

> *We are called to forgive, but we are given no guidance in working with our feelings of anger, rage, disappointment and shame.*
>
> —Sandra M. Flaherty

Roots of Anger

Often anger is rooted in hurt and fear. Hurt and fear make us feel threatened physically, emotionally, or relationally. The feeling of threat may arise from unmet need. An infant's cry becomes angry when its hunger is not satisfied. When parents do not respond appropriately to a child's growing physical or emotional needs, children experience hurt, fear, and anger. Unmet needs can occur in marriages and friendships too. Sometimes we expect one other person to meet all our needs and become angry when our impossible expectation fails us. Whether a fear is real or imagined, whether the hurt is an objective truth or a subjective perception, the feelings will be the same.

There are other sources of perceived threat to our personal wellbeing or to the people and values we hold most dear. Words and acts that humiliate, intimidate, or directly harm us may form the bedrock of our anger. Such words and acts deserve our indignation. If we know we have done something to elicit a hateful response, we may feel guilt as well as anger. But if our action triggers an outraged response though we intended no harm, we will feel misunderstood, unjustly accused, and misjudged.

Injustice is also a root of anger in this world. Twisted justice may result from prejudice, misinformation, or ignorance. It may arise from outright greed, power lust, and indifference. Feelings of outrage are valid in the face of injustice.

Ironically, those most responsible for gross violations of justice are often least willing to admit fault. Indeed, the worst abusers of human dignity routinely deny that they are unjust. Human beings are capable of massive denial, rationalization, and self-justification. Extreme national, ethnic, and religious ideologies are more likely to arise when a whole class of people feels victimized by a history of humiliation or oppression. We have seen the pattern repeated in many forms over the last century. The oppression of peasants by Russian czars led beyond revolution to the iron rule of Communism. The humiliation of the German nation after World War I cultivated a fertile seedbed for the rise of Hitler. Because the Serbian nation saw itself

> *The struggles that people feel in relation to their anger, hatred, and desires for revenge not only are real; they seem to reflect morally significant attitudes.*
>
> —L. Gregory Jones

through the historical lens of victimhood, many of its citizens were unable to acknowledge the moral horror of their genocidal policy toward Muslims in Bosnia. These are but a few examples.

People who habitually see themselves as victims do not easily recognize when they have crossed the line from being oppressed to being oppressors. They tend to see their actions in the light of self-defense or national security. The "victim mentality" prevents people from seeing how they turn the tables when power shifts in their favor. This dynamic occurs at both international and interpersonal levels.

Since anger can become so destructive, it is wise for us to look more closely at this feeling. Anger forms the link between feeling hurt and lashing back, the bridge between fear of harm and preemptive striking out. What we do with our anger can make or break human relationships, which becomes a matter of weighty consideration in a world as fragile and explosive as ours.

Types of Anger

Anger exists in differing types and degrees. At least four types are familiar to most of us: irritation, frustration, hostility, and rage. These types often follow an increasing order of intensity, although each one has its own degree of heat. In addition to these types, we might identify "outrage," or a sense of righteous indignation.

Irritation is low-level anger, often resulting from minor annoyances that grate on our sense of how things should be. If your spouse squeezes the toothpaste from the center and you roll the tube from the bottom, you may feel irritated with each other. If you spill spaghetti sauce on your white shirt, you will feel irritated with yourself. Repeated irritation can build over time to a stronger level. When a deep level of anger already resides within us over something unrelated to toothpaste or spaghetti, minor irritants can become the last straw!

Frustration, what we feel when our efforts or designs are blocked in some way, is another type of anger. Trying to control the behavior of others, particularly adolescents and grown adults, is usually an exercise in frustration. When we cannot complete an important task or make progress toward a goal, we feel frustrated. Some of the deepest frustrations occur at the level of basic relational needs, such as being unable to make ourselves heard or to elicit appreciation from others. Another source of great frustration comes from having no opportunity to exercise our best gifts. Flora S. Wuellner points out that being unable to use a true gift is like the pain of an impacted tooth. The gift remains submerged, aching to be released! We feel we cannot give birth to our deepest creativity or bear the fruit that is uniquely ours to offer others.

Hostility or outright resentment characterizes a third type of anger. We often refer to these emotions as plain "anger." We may direct such feelings outward to people we feel animosity toward, or we may direct them inward toward ourselves even when we are angry at others. Inward-directed hostility can lead to depression, despair, and physical illness. Women are more prone to turn anger in on themselves than men, since culturally women are discouraged from showing hostility. Men tend to turn their pain into anger since they are culturally discouraged from showing grief. This understanding helps to explain why men more often appear hostile than women, even when feelings beneath the surface are similar. Active hostility is hard to hide because it is accompanied by physiological responses like a rise in adrenaline and blood pressure. It generally affects our voice, facial expression, and body language. Some of us, however, have learned to disguise our anger. Covert anger is a dangerous thing. We can manage sometimes to hide it even from ourselves until it erupts in vicious responses we may later heartily regret.

Rage is often our masked tears.
—Flora Slosson Wuellner

The extreme of anger is rage, a volatile anger. Its explosiveness is physically dangerous and emotionally destructive. Rage, uncontrolled anger, can simmer below the surface of life until something triggers its boiling point. It can also be frozen into cold-blooded calculation and cunning. Frozen rage may be even more deadly than hot fury because of its surreptitious and unpredictable nature. Part of what made the terrorist attacks of September 11, 2001, so utterly chilling was the patient, icy calculation behind the rage.

The type of anger that we identify as outrage generally has the sense of justified rage or righteous indignation. It is a natural response when sacred values have been trampled or our deepest sense of morality transgressed. And here we come to an area that requires true discernment. How does righteous indignation differ from self-righteous anger? Much depends on our perspective here.

Righteous or Self-Righteous Anger?

Jesus became angry at the money changers in the Temple. He saw them profaning through commerce God's holiest dwelling among the people. It was not merely commercial interest that profaned the Temple, however, but greed and extortion that had become standard practice with the money changers. Jesus accused them of turning this sacred house of prayer into "a den of robbers" (Luke 19:46). Jesus also got upset with the scribes, Pharisees, and lawyers of Israel. He accused them of outright hypocrisy, at times listing their sins in a string of reprimands (Luke 11:37-52).

We need to understand that the Pharisaic strain of Judaism constituted the "holiness movement" of its time. The Pharisees prided themselves on keeping every aspect of God's law as written in the Torah. They fasted and prayed regularly; they tithed on everything they owned, including their garden produce. Pharisees were considered among the most righteous Jews of Israel. But Jesus called them hypocrites, which shocked and offended them deeply. They saw themselves as righteous. Jesus saw them, with few exceptions, as self-righteous.

What about us? How do we know where we stand? We are all human, susceptible to deceptions both subtle and gross. How can we know if our various types of anger are "godly" or self-centered? What criteria can help us recognize our self-deception?

The passages in Luke offer clues. Jesus' anger in the Temple expresses his deep pain that God's central law of love is being trampled. Unscrupulous people are taking advantage of ordinary folk who have come to the Temple to make sacrifices to God. The poor can only afford a pair of doves for sacrifice, but even they are overcharged in the money exchange game. Jesus makes it clear that this kind of behavior has nothing to do with worship in God's house.

As for the Pharisees, lawyers, and scribes, Jesus points out that what they teach and how they live are different realities. These leaders have become infatuated with the power and prestige of their positions in Jewish society. They have come to love the attention and deference they receive by keeping an outward show of scrupulous religiosity. So wedded to the externals of the Law are they, so intent on keeping the minutiae, that they fail to see the big picture—the demands of justice and love. They fail to comprehend that God sees the inward person. So they are blind, teaching their converts to be as tradition-bound and blind to spiritual reality as they themselves are. (See Matthew 15; 23.)

One of the keys, then, to discerning whether our anger is righteous or self-righteous rests in examining the integrity of our lives. To what extent do we live what we teach and preach? How much of our anger is rooted in pain over the hypocrisy of people who seduce, destroy, or weigh down others with teachings they do not follow themselves?

Another key to discernment is the extent to which we have within us a spirit of genuine humility. Are we so convinced of our own rightness that we feel there can be no possibility of error in our minds or hearts? In the midst of denouncing the scribes and Pharisees Jesus says pointedly, "The greatest among you will be your servant. All who exalt themselves will be humbled, and all who humble themselves will be exalted" (Matt. 23:11-12). In all things, even (or maybe especially) in our anger, there must be humility if it is to be truly righteous.

A third key to discernment raises the question, How is our anger related to our faithfulness to the great commandments: to love God with all our heart, soul, mind, and strength, and our neighbor as ourself? Is our anger rooted in a breach of love for God and neighbor? What is really at stake? What lies beneath our anger when we dig down deep?

When we begin to examine ourselves and our anger, we will discover many things. We may begin to recognize our anger's roots in wounded ego and pride. We may discover what offends our sense of morality or ethics and begin to clarify how much of the offense relates to surface-level convention as opposed to the "weightier matters" of God's justice and love. We may discern the difference between a "clear anger" that is direct and manageable and a "muddled anger" that drags in its wake the baggage of past wounds and disappointments. We may even start to see the strength and energy of our anger as a resource to be tapped for good purpose.

Facing and naming our anger offers a good place to start dealing with it. The challenge is not to get rid of this feeling but to understand why it arises and how to deal with this feeling constructively. Not anger but what we do with it is what matters. God bids us, like Cain, to master our anger so that it will not master us. When directed appropriately and handled well, even our anger can eventually move us closer to a posture of forgiveness and release.

DAILY EXERCISES

Read Week 3, "Facing Our Anger." Keep your journal at hand to record thoughts and feelings. Remember to take time for silence, turn your attention to God, and open yourself to the guidance of the Holy Spirit before each exercise. This week you will be reflecting on your own experience of anger in its various types, using various Gospel stories and Psalm 139 as aids to self-examination. Remember that honest expression and claiming God's grace are always central to seeing ourselves clearly.

EXERCISE 1

Read Psalm 139:1-6. Join the psalmist in opening your heart to God, who has known and loved you since before you were born. Ask God to help you search and find early life experiences with anger. From whom or toward whom did you experience anger? What did you learn about anger as a child? Write some of your memories or sketch images that come to mind.

In your time of prayer, open the door of your memories to Christ. Allow him to accompany you on a walk through one of your early memories. Let him see and share the whole experience. Talk the event over with him. Now see and feel for those involved through the eyes and heart of Christ. Record what happens, giving praise to God who is "acquainted with all my ways" (v. 3).

EXERCISE 2

Irritation. Read Matthew 15:21-28. The Canaanite woman's constant shouting clearly bothers the disciples. Even Jesus appears less than responsive. Yet beneath the irritating surface of this foreigner, Jesus discovers exemplary faith. What kind of human behaviors or differences commonly irritate you? What lies at the root of your irritation? In prayer, bring to mind a person or group that elicits irritation in you. Remain present to them for a while in the love of Christ. Be aware of your resistance and pay attention to what lies beneath the surface in you and in them. Note your reflections in your journal.

EXERCISE 3

Frustration. Read Matthew 23:37-39. Sadness born of love and disappointment over what could have been lies beneath Jesus' frustration over Jerusalem's inhospitable treatment of God's messengers. Identify a source of frustration in your life. Sit with your feeling for a few moments. Get in touch with where your goals are blocked or your hopes disappointed. Offer your feelings to God and explore whether it is your will or God's will that is frustrated. If it seems to be more God's will, pray for the long-suffering and patience that sustained Jesus as he persevered to fulfill his life purpose.

Read the passage again as if you were the people of Jerusalem and ask yourself, *In what ways could Jesus be lamenting me or my community? In what ways am I or are we frustrating God with our own desires? Over the years what inspirations or inner challenges has God set before me that I have disregarded?* Let your reflections guide you into prayer, and record any insights.

EXERCISE 4

Resentment. Read Luke 15:25-32. Return to the story of the elder brother who "became angry and refused to go in" to the homecoming celebration for his younger brother. What is your understanding of why he was so upset? Reread verses 29-30 and see how deeply hurt this man was. When have you been so deeply hurt and angry that you withdrew and refused to participate in the joy of another? Where does that relationship now stand?

List two or more relationships where you sometimes feel the kind of hurt or resentment that the elder son felt. Beside each relationship, write out the nature of your grievance and what it would take in your mind and heart to resolve the matter. Bring each relationship before God, whose heart goes out to both of you. Listen to the voice of God's unconditional love. Write what you hear.

EXERCISE 5

Rage/Outrage. Read Psalm 139:19-24. Get in touch with the right-eous anger that rises up within you from time to time, when you feel that you "hate those who hate" God (v. 21). Who are the "wicked" in your eyes? How have they hurt you or the people God loves? Write about the situation and your feelings.

Look at the three "keys" to discernment (see page 41). Can you assess whether your anger is righteous or self-righteous, or a mix-ture? In your time of prayer, express to Christ your anger toward those "wicked" people. Let no part of your "hate" go unexpressed to him. When you are emptied, pray "Search me, O God, and know my heart; test me and know my thoughts" (v. 23). Record your insights, expressing your anger verbally or in writing. Then release your anger, insofar as you can, to God.

Remember to review the insights recorded in your notebook or journal for the week in preparation for the group meeting.

Transforming Anger

*P*erhaps at this point we have a clearer sense of various types of anger and the dangers of mishandling this emotion. It will be good now to explore in more depth the positive side of anger, as well as how anger's negative expressions might be transformed.

Despite the suggestion in last week's article that anger in itself is value-neutral, we may still wonder if anger can have a positive effect. "The New Testament leans toward a negative view of human anger as an expression of inflamed self-seeking."[1] The letter of James encourages believers to be "slow to anger; for your anger does not produce God's righteousness" (1:19-20). And Jesus seems to imply that nursing anger against another person is just as worthy of judgment as murder! (See Matthew 5:21-22.) For Christians, anger is felt to be highly problematic in relation to faith. We tend to believe that we should not be angry, so we try to deny or suppress it in ourselves. But denying or suppressing anger cannot help us move through the process of healing and forgiveness. We must be able to acknowledge, accept, and work with all our strongest feelings if we are to move forward on this journey.

The Positive Face of Anger

It may help to begin with some specific scriptural examples of the use of anger as a tool for good. When the ancient Hebrew prophets spoke in harsh language to the Israelites of God's judgment upon them, the people were expected to hear and respond with repentance. As one writer points out, the prophets' "angry rebukes concerning the injustices of their day...shows anger as a positive force used by certain people to call others to a deeper conversion."[2] We probably have experienced this dynamic in our own lives. Sometimes a sharp rebuke wakes us up to foolishness or enables us to see the error of our thought or action. Anger can arrest us, forcing us to take stock of our words and acts.

Mark's Gospel recounts that one Sabbath Jesus was in the synagogue with a man who had a withered hand. The religious leaders watched to see if Jesus would cure the man on the Sabbath so they could accuse him of transgressing the law. One translation says that Jesus looked around at them "with anger and sorrow at their obstinate stupidity" (Mark 3:5, NEB), then proceeded to heal the man's hand. In this case, Jesus' anger served as an expression of his grief at the hardness of human hearts. It was an appropriate emotion. But instead of allowing it to carry him into angry arguments with the Pharisees, Jesus allowed the love that informed his anger to bring about the healing he intended.

In much the same way, we naturally feel anger over apparent indifference to human suffering or over decisions that carelessly create misery for others. Grieved anger can lead us to offer our time, energy, and abilities to alleviate suffering. It can impel us to find creative solutions to difficult social and ethical problems. Anger expressed in such a way has served a useful purpose.

Anger can also sustain our will to live when we find ourselves trapped in fearful, wretched, or abusive conditions. It served to keep some Jewish prisoners alive under the despicable treatment of the Nazis. Anger has kept prisoners innocent of the crimes they were accused of strong enough to fight the injustice of their sentences and has enabled desperately sick people to resist their disease with every fiber of their being. Anger can even help people who have lost their faith to wrestle with God until they discover greater depths of faith.

The gift of anger is that it locates our wound, helps us defend ourselves and energizes us to correct what needs correction.

—Dennis Linn,
Sheila Fabricant Linn,
and Matthew Linn

Therapists know that anger can be a healthy sign for people who have repressed their rage out of fear or self-hatred. Acknowledging and expressing anger quite literally begins the healing process, especially for persons who have experienced serious abuse and have felt powerless to confront the abusers. All the submerged rage, the self-blame, the feeling of entrapment and depression must come forth and be released, like draining a festering sore, before healing can take effect.

These various ways of channeling anger can release energy for life and constructive change. We are not so much called to rid ourselves of anger as to allow it to become, in some sense, a spiritual guide. What does our anger teach us? Where can it lead us if we place it in God's hands? If we listen to our anger, we will become aware of its nature and source. Once aware, we can then "evaluate it, accept responsibility for it, and find appropriate ways to express it and resolve it."[3]

Part of the process of evaluation is seeing clearly when and how anger needs to be redeemed. Sometimes our hostility does not convert readily into constructive purposes. We may need to work through our feelings and let them go. Or we may need to gain a larger perspective that puts our emotions in a different framework within which new feelings can emerge. At this point our spiritual practices play a clear role. Their purpose is to transform anger "from a devouring to an empowering force."[4] Acting in anger is rarely constructive. Acting from a clear inner center informed by anger is quite a different matter. This great principle of nonviolent action was well understood by Mohandas Gandhi and Martin Luther King Jr. And it is precisely what Jesus did with his anger toward the Pharisees when he healed the man with the withered hand.

Spiritual Practices for Transforming Anger

Several effective ways of coping with anger can help move us from being controlled by it to mastering it for good purpose. Choosing the most appropriate practice in a given situation is a matter for personal discernment. Your personality may also lead you to choose one method over another.

1. The first practice is simple attentiveness. It involves sitting *with* your anger, not on it. It means shutting your mouth and letting go of your impulse to react immediately, so you can observe what is really going on in you. Probing questions may surface as you sit with your anger and watch how it surges and subsides. Where is your anger coming from? Is it rooted in wounded pride? in a felt threat to your sense of dignity, security, or control? in your care for another's well-being? Is it attached to a long train of past wounds or complaints? Is it proportional to the offense? How does it feel in your body; where does it affect you (chest, throat, stomach, jaw)? As you attend patiently to your anger without forcing it away or judging it, its character may begin to change a bit. It may seem less urgent and demanding. You may find yourself discerning how to respond to the external situation or person causing your feelings. Through this spiritual practice of attentiveness, your anger "is first felt, then detoxified and metabolized in a non-destructive way."[5]

2. A second practice is to express your anger directly to God. We often fear that God will somehow be incensed with us if we express our anger to high heaven. But God already knows how we feel. If we truly know divine mercy, we will comprehend from the gut that God is better equipped than anyone to handle our anger. Expressing anger to God can take several forms. We may pray in bald confession, as one veteran of struggle with anger suggests: "God, I'm mad as hell, and I don't know what to do about it. I'm a wildly boiling pot, seething with violence and hatred. If you don't help me with this, no telling what I will end up doing."[6]

   The value of a prayer like this is that it faces us squarely with ourselves as we are now, a critical understanding. The destructive power of anger feeds on self-deception. We want to believe that we don't really feel such hatred or violence. We'd like to pretend that the situation isn't really so bad, and we can handle it without creating unnecessary conflict or an unpleasant scene. We want to ignore or hide our anger, a socially uncouth and "un-Christian"

Starting to pray where our hearts are, rather than where we think they ought to be, brings us closer to God.

—Jane E. Vennard

emotion. But as one wise person has recently reminded me, "God cannot find you where you think you ought to be; God can only find you where you actually are."[7] If we do not recognize where we are, we cannot fully offer ourselves to God for healing.

Another way to express anger to God is to write God a letter, as Madeleine L'Engle once did. She called it "Love Letter," and it began with the words,

> I hate you, God.
> Love, Madeleine.[8]

Her letter reveals that sometimes we not only express our anger *to* God but direct our anger *at* God. Painful situations of life can leave us feeling desperately angry with God. Our accusations come out in questions: Why did my spouse have to die so young in that plane crash? Why must my beloved sister suffer so, wasting slowly away with an agonizing disease? Why can't we conceive a baby? Why do you allow soldiers to shoot innocent civilians? God, how could you let this tragedy happen? Our best option is to express such anger and pain to God as fully and honestly as we can. Then we need to wait patiently and listen for how God may respond—in a tiny inward whisper, in the dawning of a new sense of understanding, in a changed circumstance, in a word from someone who speaks to our heart.

We might also try writing a dialogue as part of our prayer. Talk with Jesus on paper about your anger, and see how he responds in your imagination. You could try the same exercise with a favorite saint if you have a good sense of that person's deepest faith convictions. What, for example, might the apostle Paul say to you? He clearly knew anger and frustration in his ministry with various churches and directly confronted Peter over the issue of Gentile circumcision. What about Martha of Bethany, who certainly experienced irritation with her sister Mary, if not with Jesus as well! Perhaps Saint Francis would bring you fresh perspective or Saint Teresa of Avila with her remarkable humor in the midst of irritation, pain, and unjust circumstances.

Pray in any way that you can.…Bring your hurts, your sorrows, your heartbreaks, your loneliness to the Lord. If this is what you have, this must be the gift you bring to the altar.…Prayer avoids denial and brings you to face real issues.
—William A. Meninger

3. A third approach to transforming anger is to pray for our enemies. This humbling spiritual practice requires us to see the
humanity of one we might prefer to dehumanize. "There is some
bad in the best of us and some good in the worst of us."[9] To pray
for our enemies may be the best, or even the only, way to love
them. It requires us to take the other into our inner sanctum of
personal care in God's presence. Glenn Hinson expresses this profound dynamic beautifully:

> Rather than asking God to side with us,…prayer *for* another means
> to bring that person, just as he or she is, with ourselves before God
> so the rays of God's transforming love can pour over both of us, to
> transform and renew and redirect. Prayer is about love. In prayer we
> open ourselves to the love of God. We push open our doors and
> fling back our shutters and let God's love flood our inner chambers
> like the sun's rays flood a dark room.…Prayer for enemies is not a
> picnic.[10]

4. A fourth spiritual practice can help us shift gears from anger to
gratitude. This approach involves intentionally seeking goodness
in our situation. Since God is present everywhere, we will find
grace in the shadows as well as in the light. Robert Morris discovered that daily frustration could become a doorway into reg-
ular prayer. His discovery arose from a stubbed toe. After breathing
a frustrated curse, he realized that even his cursing was a stunted
expression of prayer. So he took "a second breath" and let his
prayer deepen into a genuine cry for God's blessing in the situation. As he prayed, his eyes began to open and his feelings began
to change. With time, he found many ways to turn everyday frustrations into prayer and a changed perception. Here is Morris's
description of this dynamic on one occasion:

> I stand behind a tangibly impatient woman at the local bakery. A
> dozen customers are ahead of us, and fewer salesclerks than usual.
> She sighs; she huffs; she shifts restlessly from one foot to another,
> checking the time. Her frustration agitates the air around her.…
> She may have a right to be impatient, for all I know. No doubt

*When we experience
others as enemies, we
harden our hearts
against them.…But
when we pray for
those who have hurt
us, our hearts soften
and we begin to feel
compassion.*

—Jane E. Vennard

this is not the way she planned to spend her time. We can stand on our rights all the way to hell and back, for all the good it will do us. But this ten minutes of life will never come again for either of us.…

My own annoyance takes a deep second breath. As my right hand turns palm up in an unobtrusive gesture of prayer, the sights and sounds of this friendly bakery become clearer. Two young children play happily in the nearby kiddy corner. Sunlight streams through the window behind me, warming my back. It's a wonderful place to be on a busy Saturday morning, full of wholesome goodness. My favorite Hebrew chant, *Hineni* ("Here am I"), arises in the back of my throat. The gift of standing here is simple, good, and sweet. I share that goodness with the unhappy woman, surrounding her with God's light in my heart. I can't say this makes much difference in her visible behavior, but it's better than my impatience rubbing against her impatience.[11]

We can see in this description how Morris's previous simple prayer practices came to his aid. But the first step was to recognize in this ordinary moment an invitation to see the goodness of the situation. After all, he too could have experienced the waiting time as pure frustration.

To practice gratitude, praise, and blessing in the midst of annoyance, difficulty, and suffering is one of the great spiritual disciplines. Jesus practiced it on the very night he was betrayed to a dreadful death by one of his own inner circle: He took bread and gave thanks. Looking for reasons to praise and thank God can help us gain a new attitude in the midst of anger as well.

Learning to cope constructively with hurt and anger lays the groundwork for what is perhaps the most challenging spiritual practice in human life: forgiveness. Next week we will begin to consider more directly some aspects of this difficult yet wonderfully freeing reality of the Christian life.

DAILY EXERCISES

Read Week 4, "Transforming Anger." Keep a journal of your reflections and images. Settle yourself in openness and expectancy before God as you begin each exercise. This week you will explore several ways to cope with and transform your anger through practices such as prayerful attention, listening, and giving voice to your feelings. Even your angriest feelings can be named and dealt with in ways that allow their tremendous energy to be shaped and directed for the good. Ask God to help you experience this redemptive dynamic.

EXERCISE 1

Read Psalm 69:1-5, 19-36. The psalmist's emotions range from grieved lament to outraged curses, and finally end with praise and trust. Review the past twenty-four hours (or expand the time if necessary) and become aware of your own range of emotions. Draw a time line across a page in your journal, marking the hours from our awakening to our bedtime. Beneath the time line, make notations representing actions, incidents, meetings, or surprises that made up the content of your day. Beneath those notations, indicate the attitudes or emotions you associate with each part of the day. Pay special attention to where you experienced any form of anger or irritation.

Observe the range of emotions in your life over this one day. Circle and reflect on where you handled your anger or irritation well. Also mark a place where you could have handled your anger in a more constructive way or made better use of it. Reflect on the challenge before you in allowing your anger to be transformed for good.

EXERCISE 2

Sitting with our anger. Read Luke 10:38-42. When Martha reacted to Mary's behavior by showing Jesus her hurt and angry feelings, Jesus pointed out that she was "worried and distracted by many things." Get in touch with a situation or relationship that tries your patience or stirs your anger. Rather than sitting *on* your anger, sit *with* your anger. Imagine Jesus interviewing you about the many things that bother you. What is the source of your anger? Are your needs not being met? Is your pride wounded or your dignity threatened? Are you envious? What is the deeper history behind this issue? "There is need of only one thing," said Jesus. Spend some time getting clear about "the one thing needed" in your life, and see how that clarity influences your relationship to the situation. Record your thoughts.

EXERCISE 3

Expressing anger directly to God. Read Numbers 11:10-15. As the children of Israel complained about their misfortunes, the Lord became angry. Moses, in turn, became "displeased" with God and directly accused God of treating him badly. When have you become intensely displeased with God? Perhaps part of you is displeased with the way God made you, the harshness with which life has treated you or a loved one, or life's injustice toward others in the larger world. Rather than carry your complaint in secret, do as the saints before you have done: Tell God. Write a letter or speech expressing your displeasure with God in raw honesty. Hold God accountable for what God has created or allowed to happen. Empty your heart of your complaint. As you write, pause on occasion and listen for God's reply. Notice that God responds to Moses' honesty with a creative solution. (See verses 16-17.)

EXERCISE 4

Praying for enemies. Read Matthew 5:43-48. Follow Jesus into an experiment in faith: Pray for those who anger you rather than curse them. Select a person now with whom you have particular trouble and decide to apply your mind to God's goodwill for him or her. Don't attempt to change your feelings; simply focus elsewhere—on God's love for this person. When you become distracted, return in your mind to God's love and let old, angry thoughts subside. Practice this approach throughout the day. Create a short, one-sentence prayer (often called a "breath prayer") to help you keep your focus, for example, "Lord, thy will be done in Sally's life," or "Create in me a clean heart, O God." (See the guidelines for "Developing Your Breath

Prayer" on pages 57–58.) Beginning today, make a record of your experience.

EXERCISE 5

Seeking goodness. Read Philippians 4:4-9. The apostle Paul challenges us to make a practice of rejoicing in every circumstance, continually turning our minds to whatever is true, honorable, and just. Consider when and where you have cursed a situation in angry words or force of feeling. Reflect on how you could have deliberately turned your angry reaction into a redemptive response, the curses ("Gosh darn!") into blessings ("God bless!"). Note insights in your journal. Over the next twenty-four hours, pay attention to every time you react in a damning way to situations that displease you. At such times, practice taking a "second breath" by turning your curse into a blessing for what God has given you with a clear intent to bring out the good in the situation. Record your adventure.

Remember to review the insights recorded in your notebook or journal for the week in preparation for the group meeting.

Developing Your Breath Prayer

The breath prayer is an ancient way of practicing the presence of God. It is a way to cultivate a posture of constant awareness and availability toward God.

Like prayers of repetition, breath prayers can be phrases from tradition, scripture, or hymnody. We repeat these phrases with our lips, carry them in our hearts, and whisper them under our breath.

The breath prayer is a way to act on your decision to be present to God, who is always present to us. Practice your breath prayer at special times when you give God your undivided attention. Continue to say your breath prayer under your breath; let it become a habit of the heart.

Spend a few minutes now in developing and praying your breath prayer. Write it down as a reminder to keep with your journal.

Ron DelBene (pronounced like bane), a contemporary author of books on the spiritual life, has written extensively on creating and using personal breath prayers. The following steps are taken from his book *The Breath of Life: A Workbook*.

STEP ONE
Sit in a comfortable position. Close your eyes, and remind yourself that God loves you and that you are in God's loving presence. Recall a passage from scripture that puts you in a prayerful frame of mind. Consider "The Lord is my shepherd" (Psalm 23:1) or "Be still, and know that I am God!" (Psalm 46:10).

STEP TWO
With your eyes closed, imagine that God is calling you by name. Hear God asking, "(*Your name*), what do you want?"

STEP THREE
Answer God with whatever comes directly from your heart. Your answer might be a single word, such as *peace* or *love* or *forgiveness*. Your answer could instead be a phrase or brief sentence, such as "I want to feel your forgiveness" or "I want to know your love."

Because the prayer is personal, it naturally rises out of our present concerns.... Your response to God's question "What do you want?" becomes the heart of your prayer.

STEP FOUR

Choose your favorite name or image for God. Choices commonly made include God, Jesus, Creator, Teacher, Light, Lord, Spirit, Shepherd.

STEP FIVE

Combine your name for God with your answer to God's question "What do you want?" You then have your prayer. For example:

What I Want	Name I Call God	Possible Prayer
peace	God	Let me know your peace, O God.
love	Jesus	Jesus, let me feel your love.
rest	Shepherd	My Shepherd, let me rest in thee.
guidance	Eternal Light	Eternal Light, guide me in your way.

What do you do if several ideas occur? Write down the various possibilities and then eliminate and/or combine ideas until you have focused your prayer. You may want many things, but it is possible to narrow wants to those most basic to your well-being. Thus, the question to ask yourself is *What do I want that will make me feel most whole?* As you achieve a greater feeling of wholeness, serenity will flow into the many areas of your life.

When you have gotten to the heart of your deep yearning, search for words that give it expression. Then work with the words until you have a prayer of six to eight syllables that flows smoothly when spoken aloud or expressed as a heart thought. A prayer of six to eight syllables has a natural rhythm. Anything longer or shorter usually does not flow easily when said repeatedly. Some prayers are more rhythmic when you place God's name at the beginning; other prayers flow better with it at the end.

Ron DelBene, Herb Montgomery, and Mary Montgomery, *The Breath of Life: A Workbook* (Nashville, Tenn.: Upper Room Books, 1996), 12–13. Used by permission of Upper Room Books.

Week 5

Receiving God's Forgiveness

*N*ow we are in a position to bring what we are learning about blessedness and anger directly into our reflections on forgiveness, a thorny rose with a heavenly fragrance. Spiritually speaking, forgiveness is a thing of incomparable beauty. But our difficulties with forgiveness—theologically, emotionally, and practically—are prickly matters that can cause discomfort if not significant pain.

Just what is forgiveness? Are we required to forgive everyone who harms us? Aren't there some particularly dreadful acts that should never be forgiven? Does forgiveness depend on repentance? How does mercy fit with justice? How do we make real the ideal of forgiving others or ourselves? These questions are but a few of many that confront us when we begin to deal closely with this subject.

Forgiveness is a door to peace and happiness. It is a small, narrow door, and cannot be entered without stooping.

—Johann C. Arnold

What Is Forgiveness?

Before we try to define or clarify what forgiveness *is*, let us lay aside some of the things it is *not*. For example, to forgive does not mean to deny our hurt. Sometimes we think we are "keeping the peace" and showing a forgiving attitude when all we have done is suppress our pain. Forgiveness is possible only when we acknowledge the hurtful impact of a person's actions on our lives, whether or not the offender intended harm.

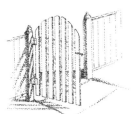

Accepting inappropriate blame for our hurt is a close cousin of denying our hurt. A person with a weak sense of self or an inflated sense of responsibility easily takes the blame for others' actions. "It's my fault that I got hurt. I must have done something to invite this." If we believe that we are the source of our own pain or that we deserve to be degraded and abused, we again have disguised the offense that needs forgiving by taking false responsibility for it. Resignation to the role of victim will prevent any genuine process of forgiveness.

Forgiveness is not merely a feeling. It is a disposition of our whole person, a habit of the heart, intentional choices of action in relationship. It does not involve trying to manipulate ourselves or others into feeling forgiven or forgiving.

Neither is forgiveness a commodity we can purchase through fervent repentance. We cannot earn it simply by showing that we are thoroughly ashamed of ourselves. Creating melodramas around forgiveness can easily lead us into self-deception and false piety.

Writer Anthony Bloom has astutely pointed out that forgiveness does not mean "putting someone on probation." We may think we have forgiven a person only to catch ourselves waiting impatiently for evidence that the person's behavior merits our clemency. If the offender doesn't measure up, the "gift" of mercy is withdrawn. "To grant forgiveness at a moment of softening of the heart, in an emotional crisis, is comparatively easy," says Bloom. "Not to take it back is something that hardly anyone knows how to do."[1]

Perhaps the most pernicious block to forgiveness comes in the erroneous idea that to forgive is to *excuse*. Our sense of fairness, our convictions about justice, our need to hold persons accountable for their behaviors all argue strongly against excusing harmful attitudes and actions. Evil ideologies and destructive behaviors are inherently inexcusable. Fraud, theft, violence, abuse, exploitation, denial of basic human rights—who would ever claim these are excusable? Excusing such behaviors condones them. Forgiving is not tolerating the intolerable. Yet we can forgive a *person* whose *actions* remain condemned. Distinguishing between the person and the act is crucial to the integrity of forgiveness.

Much of what passes for Christian forgiveness is simply a denial of hurt and anger.
—C. Gordon Peerman III

Finally, forgiving is not necessarily forgetting. Perhaps for small indignities that prick our pride we can simply excuse and forget. But for major assaults that leave us gasping for breath, reeling with rejection, bowing under oppression, or aching with loss and grief we will find ourselves unable to forget. In some situations it is not desirable to forget. It would be further arrogance for people of European descent to ask Native or African Americans, under the guise of forgiveness, to forget the history of their shameful oppression in this country. Our Jewish friends rightly insist that we never forget the horrors of the Holocaust. Some things must be well remembered if we are to find our way to a life-giving future. Some things cannot, humanly speaking, be forgotten. However, the people involved may over time be forgiven.

Acts of cruelty and evil cannot be condoned or forgiven.... When we are the victims of radical evil, we are not asked to forgive the evil act. We are asked to remember that the perpetrator, even though trapped for now in the evil, is nonetheless a child of God.
—Flora Slosson Wuellner

If we now have a clearer sense of the "false coin" of forgiveness, what is the genuine article? Here are a few possible descriptions of this particular flowering of the Spirit:

> Forgiveness is what happens when the victim of some hurtful action freely chooses to release the perpetrator of that action from the bondage of guilt, gives up his or her own feelings of ill will, and surrenders any attempt to hurt or damage the perpetrator in return, thus clearing the way for reconciliation and restoration of relationship.[2]

> To forgive is to make a conscious choice to release the person who has wounded us from the sentence of our judgment, however justified that judgment may be. It represents a choice to leave behind our resentment and desire for retribution, however fair such punishment might seem.[3]

> Forgiveness is taking responsibility from my side to release the offender from the alienating effect of the offense on our relationship.[4]

No single definition or characterization of forgiveness seems quite adequate, for the flower of forgiveness has many petals and takes different shapes in different situations. Scholar Gregory Jones notes that "one of the most offensive things Christians all too often do is to proclaim a general and abstract forgiveness without any regard for the complexities of a specific situation or a particular person's life."[5] Forgiveness might be quite differently expressed in a situation where someone hits another person once in a fit of anger as opposed to the case of someone who habitually strikes another.

Our limited understanding of forgiveness and our flawed practice of this blessing would encourage us to root ourselves in scripture and theology. "Forgiveness is the mind of God, the life of God."[6] We will more likely find our feet on solid ground if we begin with God's forgiveness of us than if we start with our effort to forgive others.

God's Forgiveness of Us

To forgive others the sins they commit against us is not our first task. First we receive the forgiveness God offers for the sins we commit. Just as "we love because he first loved us" (1 John 4:19), so we can only forgive because we have first been forgiven. If we do not know what it means to be forgiven, how can we possibly extend the gift to others? Conversely, once we know from the heart what it is to be forgiven by God, how can we refuse to extend the gift to others? The totally gracious, unaccountably generous love of God is the only foundation in our faith for an exploration of human forgiveness.

Of course, in order to receive God's forgiveness we must first be aware that we need it. We need to see sin for what it is—a breach of our relationship with God, a breaking of the trust God placed in us by making covenant love the center of our life together. Scripture makes it clear that sin against God is the root of all division, all alienation. Sin is the pervasively toxic condition of human life that we are born into, absorb, and pass on to others. It is our worldliness, our wounded pride and reactive anger, our compulsive desire to control and dominate, our greed for more than we need, our hardness of heart toward fellow human beings, our need to hide from truth, our willingness to distort reality for our own purposes.

Sin takes a thousand forms, subtle and overt. In all kinds of ways we sin against God, others, and ourselves. Indeed, these three are virtually impossible to separate. When I fail to worship and praise God or to allow my efforts to depend on grace, I not only sin against the

God's forgiveness flows out of the richness of God's own life and seeks to share that richness with others.
—L. William Countryman

gracious, praiseworthy love of God but set myself up for controlling interactions with others. When I berate or dismiss another person, I injure the heart of Christ and diminish my own capacity for love. When I devalue myself, I insult the One who made me in the divine image and invite others to belittle me. When I elevate myself above others, I push God out of my way and feel free to use others wrongly. Every form of sin impacts all three relationships because we are designed to be in communion with one another.

We need to see our own culpability in the tangle of broken and disordered relationships from which we all suffer as well as participate in both wittingly and unwittingly. We need to become conscious of our guilt both for sins of commission and for sins of omission. None of us can escape this truth of our wounded and wounding human condition. We hurt others intentionally and unintentionally. We all have our own peculiar combination of ignorance, blindness, fear, and egotistic pride that shapes our thoughts, words, choices, and acts.

If we do not take personal sin seriously, forgiveness will have no real meaning. God takes our sin very seriously. Sin is an affront to divine goodness, justice, and holiness. Purity and truth constrain God to judge, restrain, and reeducate us. Certainly the Just One judges our sin. We have not well understood that God's judgment is always in the service of love. Love yearns to restore our relationship to the communion God intended from the beginning.

Christians believe that the ultimate judgment of our sin comes in the form of Jesus of Nazareth, crucified. "For our sake he made him to be sin who knew no sin, so that in him we might become the righteousness of God" (2 Cor. 5:21). From the cross, where human sin is dreadfully and decisively judged, Jesus prays, "Father, forgive them; for they do not know what they are doing" (Luke 23:34). Some have argued that Jesus does not directly forgive those who tortured and executed him, asking instead that God the Father do so. But Jesus makes it clear that he and the Father are one (see John 14:8-11) and that their wills are completely united in love (see Luke 22:42). In

asking the Father to forgive, Jesus indicates his own willingness to forgive. So Christ is "the judge whose judgment does not condemn but brings salvation."[7]

Divine judgment is a judgment of grace because God has a long view of the divine reign in mind. God desires not merely to mend the past but to create a new future through forgiveness. "People are mistaken if they think of Christian forgiveness primarily as absolution from guilt; the purpose of forgiveness is the restoration of communion, the reconciliation of brokenness."[8] In the person of Jesus Christ, this communion and reconciliation are already present and available. He *is* the "new creation," and in him we too are made new!

The real question then is not whether God has indeed forgiven us, for in Christ the gift is extended to all. The question is whether or not we have *received* the gift. Have we really allowed ourselves to take in the freedom and release offered to us through God's forgiveness in Christ? If so, the gift will make a visible, visceral difference in our lives and relationships. And if we cannot forgive ourselves for serious mistakes we have made, surely that signals our inability truly to accept God's forgiveness. We hold out for higher standards than God's, stuck in useless guilt. We could lift up many such stories.

God's goodness is pure gift, going radically beyond anything we have earned either by good behavior or by repentance.
—L. William Countryman

What of the man who for years verbally belittled his wife in subtle ways disguised with snide humor? With the help of a friend, he finally recognized what he was doing and repented in the true sense of turning around and changing his habits. He received his wife's forgiveness but still has not fully forgiven himself for his words and actions all those years. Whenever he recalls those behaviors he once indulged in with such ease, he sees an image of himself that he despises.

What of the woman who, not seeing her toddler behind the van when she backed out of the driveway, ran over her own child? Although she did not intend to harm her little boy, she cannot forgive herself for her role in this tragedy. If only she had looked more carefully, if only she had been sure that her child was safely out of the way before starting the car!

What of the war veteran who served in Vietnam and planned napalm attacks that burned hundreds of innocent villagers? Like many such veterans, he lives daily with a terrible weight of unresolved guilt, anguish, and depression. He can find no peace of soul.

Perhaps we too suffer from guilt and remorse that, like an infected sore, will not heal. In such cases, the only remedy is to confess our sin openly and honestly. In every circumstance we can confess to God. Where possible, it helps to confess to those we have harmed. Where this is not possible, we may find relief in confessing to a minister, priest, or mature spiritual friend. Simply saying the words aloud, divulging the deepest darkness of our hearts, has a stringent healing effect. It may feel very shameful, painful, or humiliating, but such confession serves as the beginning of our relief and salvation.

There is, however, a further step in taking hold of forgiveness. The Quaker writer Douglas Steere speaks to our difficulty in receiving grace with all its undercurrents of pride, anxiety, and control:

> There is…a condition for receiving God's gift of forgiveness. [We] must be willing to accept it. Absurd as this may seem, there are few who will believe in and accept the forgiveness of God so completely as to…leave their sin with God forever. They are always reopening the vault where they have deposited their sin,…forever asking to have it back in order to fondle it; reconstruct, query, or worry over it.…Thus their sin ties them to the past.[9]

When stuck in recurring guilt and self-condemnation, we become susceptible to one of two errors: judging others as harshly as ourselves or discounting ourselves and idealizing others. The Great Commandment speaks simply to this problem. It calls us to love our neighbor as ourself. If we do not love ourselves appropriately, our neighbor will not benefit much! As one wise writer puts it, "Embracing forgiveness turns out, strangely enough, to be an act of *repentance*, because it means giving up our own way of seeing the world and accepting in its place God's rather more generous way."[10]

When we seriously face the reality of our sin, the painful healing of confessing and repenting, and the humbling freedom of receiving God's forgiveness, we are then in a good position to look at the challenge of forgiving others, the subject we will turn to next week.

You shall love the Lord your God with all your heart, and with all your soul, and with all your mind.

—Matthew 22:37

DAILY EXERCISES

Special note: Spend some time this week looking for stories of forgiveness and reconciliation in books, magazines, newspapers, and in conversations with others. Bring them to the weekly group meeting this week and in the weeks remaining.

Before you begin the exercises, remember to read Week 5, "Receiving God's Forgiveness." Capture your reflections, questions, and feelings in your journal. This week you will begin to look directly at the nature of forgiveness, your need for it, and your possible resistance to receiving it fully. Such examination can be a tender and painful process but very freeing as well. Remember to settle yourself in God's presence before each exercise; then invite the grace of the Spirit to dwell in and guide you.

EXERCISE 1

Read Jeremiah 31:31-34. This passage tells us that God will write the new covenant made with Israel, not on stone tablets but on human hearts. The covenant moves from an external law to the internal knowledge of God's ways, always holding together promise and command, gift and response, in a binding agreement. Ponder what you have internalized of God's promises and commands. Write down the "covenant" you know by faith, the understanding written on your heart of how God gifts you and calls you to live.

Take time to review your life in light of this internalized covenant. Share with the Lord where you feel you are doing well and where you feel you are falling short. Ask the Lord to show you what you might not notice in either area. Then take the last sentence of verse 34 to heart. Offer thanks to God for forgiveness where you fall short and for strength where you are faithful to the covenant in your heart.

EXERCISE 2

Read Luke 15:11-32 Spend a few moments contemplating (in the story and Rembrandt painting) the image of the father running to embrace the younger son. Internalize the picture, locating your need for grace in this scene. See yourself allowing God to approach you in love and embrace your whole person despite your sin. Is there a speech of repentance, explanation, or self-justification that you feel compelled to make? Make it, but ponder what it means for your relationship with God that the father's eagerness to love the child does not wait on the repentance speech.

Give yourself to prayer for several minutes, visualizing yourself as the recipient of grace in the scene of the father welcoming the younger son. Practice receiving the sheer gift of God's forgiving love and unrestrained joy over you. Take note in your journal of anything that rises up in you to resist the gift or divert your attention. Respond to each diversion by returning again and again to the image of God's all-embracing love of you as a son or daughter of God. Draw a picture of what you see.

EXERCISE 3

Read Hosea 11:1-9. Hosea gives voice to the heartfelt plea of the Divine Lover whose motherly care and longing for relationship with Israel are repeatedly spurned. Allow the verses to guide you in contemplating the many forms of God's care and guidance throughout your life. When have you recognized God leading you "with cords of human kindness, with bands of love"? In what ways have you spurned divine love, even though it continues to reach out and sustain you?

Try to take in how foolishly in love with you God is, whose "heart recoils" at the thought of losing you and whose "compassion grows warm and tender" even in your waywardness. Spend a few minutes simply enjoying a mental picture of what it could mean for you to give up your agenda, to give in to God's all-forgiving compassion, and to give yourself over to the leading of Christ's love. Record your thoughts and images.

EXERCISE 4

Read John 8:1-11. Imagine yourself in the position of this woman, "caught" in sin of your own kind and made to "stand before all." What

accusations do you hear from within yourself, others, or God? What punishment do you fear or feel you deserve? Now listen to Jesus' words to the woman as words spoken to you: "Neither do I condemn you. Go your way, and from now on do not sin again."

What past sins continue to condemn you in your heart? Bring to mind the memories while meditating on Jesus' words, repeating them as often as you need to. Let Jesus' assurance penetrate your heart and speak to the inner accusers. Let Jesus' call, "Go your way, and…do not sin again," lead you in examining how you could allow God's love to alter your life in grace and freedom. Record your insights.

EXERCISE 5

Read 1 John 1:1-10. John's words invite us to "walk in the light" with Jesus Christ "so that our joy may be complete." Bring yourself into the cleansing light of truth by taking a mental walk through the "interior castle" of your life. Imagine the many rooms you associate with various dimensions of your life (space for work, home, church, and leisure time). Notice the rooms that are illumined by sunlight, open to the flow of fresh air and available for fellowship. Take note also of the rooms you keep off-limits or leave untended; rooms that feel dark, musty, or full of ghosts from the past. Allow Jesus Christ to walk with you in and out of every room. Let him help you see what you've accumulated, clear out obstacles, and prepare the space for "fellowship with one another" in the light of truth.

Record your discoveries. Consider what it would mean to open the castle of your heart to Christ daily, trusting that "he who is faithful and just will forgive us our sins and cleanse us from all unrighteousness."

Remember to review the insights recorded in your notebook or journal for the week in preparation for the group meeting.

Week 6
Forgiving Others

Forgiveness is God's most astonishing response to human sin. It is the only response that could give hope for a new life. That same hope enables us to envision a new future in our relationships with others who have wounded or offended us. Here we begin to consider our forgiveness of one another, tricky and difficult terrain.

In God's heart, "mercy triumphs over judgment" (James 2:13). More precisely, judgment in the service of love is merciful because God wants to restore sinners to life by all possible righteous means. This seems a welcome and good thing when we ourselves stand before God's judgment. But divine mercy does not always feel like good news when we look at other people's sins, especially those that appear much more terrible than ours!

It is the emotional side of human life that makes forgiveness so difficult. Even a strong appreciation of what God has done for us in Christ does not translate easily into forgiving others. The spouse who abandoned me, the parent who neglected me, the leader who betrayed my trust—each situation carries a history of emotional freight. We may know what we ought ultimately to do but find ourselves unable or unwilling to do it. A story from the ancient wisdom of the desert may instruct us here:

> Certain of the brethren said to Abbot Anthony: We would like you to tell us some word, by which we may be saved. Then the elder said: You

Forgiveness is the name of love practiced among people who love poorly.
—Henri J. M. Nouwen

have heard the Scriptures, they ought to be enough for you. But they said: We want to hear something also from you, Father. The elder answered them: You have heard the Lord say: If a man strikes you on the left cheek, show him also the other one. They said to him: This we cannot do. He said to them: If you can't turn the other cheek, at least take it patiently on one of them. They replied: We can't do that either. He said: If you cannot even do that, at least do not go striking others more than you would want them to strike you. They said: We cannot do this either. Then the elder said to his disciple: Go cook up some food for these brethren, for they are very weak. Finally he said to them: If you cannot even do this, how can I help you? All I can do is pray.[1]

With telling humor, this story reveals how hard it is to comprehend, much less follow, Jesus. When someone strikes us, our first impulse is to strike back. We may limit our retaliation to reasonable and proportionate punishment, to execute justice and deter further aggression. But if we feel threatened enough, we may feel compelled to counterattack with greater force or even to destroy our enemy. To ensure that the source of danger is decisively dealt with, we may then greatly multiply the injury in return. This approach is the classic root of escalating violence. We can see it on any playground, as well as in national and international politics. It's a long way from the life and teachings of Jesus.

If we have a little more maturity and self-control, we might refuse to respond in kind. Perhaps to keep things from going from bad to worse, we simply choose to suffer the blow. Maybe the offender and the offended need to talk something through to arrive at a better mutual understanding. Perhaps we need to be a lightning rod for someone at a given moment and not bother with self-defense or argument. Maybe we need to avoid a certain person in the future. Such non-retaliation may take the offender by surprise and invite further reflection. At best, it will halt aggressive behavior. But if a bully reads patience as a sign of weakness, we risk being taken advantage of.

The story of Abbot Anthony reveals a third possible response, the one proposed first by the elder. To offer the other cheek is a counsel to "overcome evil with good"(Rom. 12:21). Responding in this way requires a perceptual shift on our part. It does not come naturally when we are hurt by another. Indeed, to offer *more* of yourself to your attacker would seem positively unhealthy by psychological norms. To return good for evil, to bless and not curse your enemies—these may seem like pious platitudes for fragile souls who succumb easily to evil or aspire naively to sainthood! Of course, turning the other cheek can reflect such distortions. Everything depends on the spirit we bring to the act.

We need to understand the cultural context in which Jesus spoke of "turning the other cheek" and "walking the second mile" (Matt. 5:38-42). Notice that Jesus specifies a situation where a person has been struck on the *right* cheek. This would require the perpetrator to strike with the palm of the left hand, which was used for unclean tasks including striking a person considered inferior (using the back of the right hand was equally a sign of contempt). Turning the left cheek invites the perpetrator to strike with the palm of the right hand, which signifies that the one struck is an equal or worthy opponent. Far from making oneself a groveling doormat, the choice to turn the other cheek represents an assertion of nonviolent power and self-respect, which is the character of healthy forgiveness. Rarely do we achieve such self-possessed freedom right away.

The experience of being unfairly or badly treated leaves us justifiably hurt and angry. As discussed earlier, we need to express our hurt and anger in ways that do not harm others or ourselves. The Psalms provide a wonderful resource here. They give us permission to express every conceivable human emotion in terms as strong and undisguised as we choose. Psalms of lament can help us give voice to our grief and anguish. Psalms of "imprecation" (invoking evil upon another) can give us language for inviting God's curses upon the enemy. While this may not feel like a particularly Christian thing to do, it allows us to express with utter honesty the feelings of hatred, hostility, and helplessness that we sometimes feel when we have been wronged.

It is helpful to think of forgiveness as a journey undertaken in hope, in company with God's guiding Spirit. We can suspend the

The person who turns the other cheek is saying, in effect, "Try again. Your first blow failed to achieve its intended effect. I deny you the power to humiliate me."

—Walter Wink

notion that forgiveness is always accomplished by a simple word of pardon or a single act of the will. Learning to forgive can take a significant amount of time even if we want to do it quickly. More often than not, rapid pronouncements of forgiveness are like unripe fruit, having no sweetness or nourishment in them. They are neither fully formed nor quite real because we haven't worked through any inner process of change. Lasting forgiveness is embedded in the learning of a whole new way of life in Christ. It is connected to attitudes and practices like truthfulness, humility, perseverance, generosity of spirit, and compassion. We must learn to walk in freedom just as a child learns to walk.

In the process of learning to forgive, we may move through several stages, feelings, and behaviors in relation to the offender. These movements are by no means the same for everyone. Much depends on the nature and felt intensity of the offense, the character of the relationship prior to the offense, and our own relative spiritual and emotional maturity. We may feel stunned into withdrawal and numbness. We may move through intense anger with fantasies of revenge that we later feel guilty about. We may search desperately within ourselves for some explanation as to why we were badly treated. We may punish the offender obliquely through passive aggression, manipulation, or deceit. We may punish the other by withdrawing from the relationship. (Of course, in cases of a persistently destructive relationship, withdrawal is completely appropriate and necessary.) We may wait for an expected apology or restitution or both. This expectation is not unreasonable, and some kind of contrition in the offender's response generally helps us move toward forgiveness.

We grow by increments and should not expect ourselves to walk before learning to crawl. To begin thinking about forgiveness by focusing on an especially horrifying crisis is not very helpful. We need to start by learning to forgive the minor infractions that occur in the rub of daily life.

Author Wendy Wright relates an incident of "ruptured love restored" with her husband. About four years into their marriage, they had a heated quarrel over a minor matter. The cause was not

Lingering anger usually indicates we moved too quickly through the forgiveness process.

—Dennis Linn,
Sheila Fabricant Linn,
and Matthew Linn

particularly memorable, but the argument was, in part because they didn't often erupt at each other. She writes,

> At its most fevered pitch, he stalked out the door. I, enraged at his exit, slammed the door behind him at just the moment he decided to stalk back in. His finger got caught in the door swinging toward him. Shocked by our own vehemence and stunned into recognizing the stupidity of our quarrel, we hurried off to have his finger bound up. About a month later he wrote me a poem, a love poem of forgiveness and praise which ended with the words: "I might still be running, no crack in the door, if that flesh hadn't reached for you, and you, love, caught it."[2]

From small incidents of forgiveness like this one we gradually develop new habits that allow us to begin to see persons in fresh ways. Sometimes circumstances simply open our eyes to perspectives we had never considered before. A woman named Ellen had her eyes opened in a single night of crisis.[3]

Ellen had found her alcoholic brother Jerry harder to stand at every family gathering. Years ago he had especially infuriated her by taking their mother's piano to *his* home after their mother's death; he wanted it for his wife. But Ellen was the only one in the family who could play it, and she had always assumed it would come to her. The last she had seen it, one of Jerry's cigarettes had scarred the piano's beautiful mahogany finish. She swore she would never speak to him again. Then one midnight he had called, voice panic-stricken. Their house was on fire. Passed out from drinking, he had let his cigarette fall into the carpet. Ellen arrived just in time to watch two firemen push a smoldering piano from the front door. Her brother, who had just confessed to her how scared he was about his drinking, saw her gaze fixed on the piano. His eyes filled with tears. "Isn't it awful?" he choked. "Like losing Mom all over again. I sometimes think the only time I was ever happy was when I sat and listened to the music she made."

Ellen had never fully realized how unhappy her brother was growing up, nor did she have any idea what the piano had meant to him. This crisis brought out his deep, unexpressed feelings. It gave his sister a new perspective on the suffering behind Jerry's obnoxious behavior.

Perhaps the hardest thing about practicing forgiveness in daily life is that it requires us to confront the reality of our feelings toward those we know best.

—Johann C. Arnold

Ellen looked at him and saw the wide-eyed boy behind the puffy, creased face. With surprise she heard her own voice saying, "I've missed you."

Sometimes the resistance of our heart to another person melts away suddenly and surprisingly because a whole new picture of the situation that caused our hurt has emerged. There is so much we do not see and cannot know about those who wound us, even in our families. It is one reason we need to find ways to tell our deep stories and to hear one another's deep stories. It also reveals why we do well to leave judgment to the searcher of all hearts, who comprehends the internal as well as external realities of each situation.

This story does not state whether Ellen actually forgave her brother. What we see is that she came to a different perspective from glimpsing her brother's pain. Understanding is not the same as forgiveness, although it can set the stage for it. People do what they do for many reasons. Reasons are not excuses, but they may help us release our emotional blocks to a more merciful response. In this story, the way is open once again for a new quality of relationship between Ellen and Jerry, which is what forgiveness aims for.

These stories show aspects of forgiveness in the midst of normal family tensions and conflicts. Graver situations where a person has been traumatically or chronically victimized by violence will require significant time for emotional healing before the victim can even consider the possibility of real forgiveness.

For example, where women and children have experienced physical or sexual abuse or where the power relationship between victim and victimizer differs vastly, the abused are counseled not to rush into forgiveness. Forgiving can be glib or premature both for victim and victimizer. Almost invariably victims need time and help to grow into a stronger, more mature sense of self—a self that does not crumple in subservience to abuse and does not accept inappropriate blame for others' actions. Moreover, the perpetrators of physical violence and abuse have learned that they can be *forgiven* too quickly, before they have felt genuine remorse or learned to hold themselves accountable for their acts. Thus the force of forgiveness has been lost on them,

and they have been unable to take it in as a healing balm or life-transforming power.

We need to be tender and patient with persons deeply wounded, and with ourselves if we have been so abused. Much pain, grief, and rage will need to be worked through and let go. Again, praying the psalms or writing our own psalms can help greatly (in conjunction with good therapy). We may also find it useful to express our feelings verbally, in writing, through physical movement, artistic expression, creative play, or other forms of prayer. However, many psychotherapists now encourage clients to find a deeper level of healing through forgiveness itself. The healing that can occur without forgiving has its limits. Forgiveness brings a level of health and joy that most therapies can only approximate.

The depth-psychology perspective on forgiveness tends to focus on the personal freedom of the one who forgives. Such freedom is indeed a profound gift of healing and empowerment. We experience great benefit in being able to forgive. It releases us from carrying the corrosive effect of anger and bitterness in our own souls, and peace of soul is not an insignificant matter. Forgiveness also empowers us, allowing us to reassert our choice to become whole instead of merely accepting the diminishment of our wounds. Thus healthy forgiveness is like the original meaning of Jesus' counsel to turn the other cheek. Robert Muller, former assistant secretary-general of the United Nations, understood this when he wrote these words for International Forgiveness Week:

> Be the first to forgive,...
> For by forgiving
> You become the master of fate
> The fashioner of life
> The doer of miracles.[4]

Another writer pondered this theme following Pope John Paul II's visit to the man who had tried to assassinate him:

> Not to forgive is to yield oneself to another's control..., locked into
> a sequence of act and response, of outrage and revenge....The

Forgiveness doesn't consist of soft-headedness. It is not a way of denying, ignoring, condoning, or tolerating wrong. It begins by recognizing and naming the wrongdoing and, if at all possible, bringing it to a halt.
—L. William Countryman

present is endlessly overwhelmed and devoured by the past. Forgiveness frees the forgiver. It extracts the forgiver from someone else's nightmare.[5]

While forgiving frees the forgiver in many healthy ways, as persons of faith we surely hope that our motives in this practice go beyond self-healing. For Christians, forgiveness can never be merely therapeutic in a psychological sense. It also contains within itself the power of transformation and promise of God's redemption for the other person. We will explore these matters further in upcoming weeks.

As we learn more about the hidden depths of our heart—where we are wounded, how hard the scars are, where our pride is invested in being right or in wielding influence—our capacity for mercy grows. Forgiveness issues from a heart that has been expanded somehow by God's grace. It requires us to respond in a new way to the one who wounded us, asking us to reach across the gap of estrangement with words or gestures of reconciliation. Forgiveness invites us to reopen closed doors of communication, to write a love poem, or to extend a hand in friendship once more.

Those who practice the grace-full art of forgiveness know increasing joy and freedom in their relationships. Forgiveness is one of the eminent signs of the vitality of the Holy Spirit in our midst. The Spirit ever plays the flute within, inviting us to dance to its tune. The Spirit keeps nudging the image of God hid deep in the soul, reshaping it to look more like the one who fashioned it. The Spirit breathes possibility into impossibility and authorizes us to forgive as God forgives. Through the Holy Spirit we abide in Christ and Christ in us. What privilege, what gift!

The fuel of bitterness is always expended in vain. But...the love of a forgiving heart is never wasted.

—Johann C. Arnold

DAILY EXERCISES

Read Week 6, "Forgiving Others." Note your insights, questions, and reflections in your journal. As you begin your inner work around forgiving others, it will be especially important to take time before each exercise to center yourself in God's strong and loving presence. Remember that you cannot force yourself to forgive, since it would not then be authentic. Yet you can accept the challenge to move forward from an unforgiving spirit to a new place of mind and heart that may prepare you better to forgive in the future.

EXERCISE 1

Read Matthew 6:9-15. Jesus' strong emphasis on forgiveness in the Lord's Prayer and elsewhere calls us to be as pragmatic in assessing "our debtors" in the spirit as in our financial relationships. Make a "forgiveness list." Include all the debtors you can think of, all those persons you feel owe you something—an apology, compensation, their reputation, or their very life—for the way they hurt you or someone you love. Beside each name, note what you think he or she owes you.

Return to the Lord's Prayer. Dwell on the promise that God will "forgive us our debts, as we also have forgiven our debtors." Weigh the options before you: "a pound of flesh" from your debtors or God's peace in your heart. Begin the process of forgiving by praying for the *desire* to forgive in each case. Keep a record of your progress.

EXERCISE 2

Read Ephesians 4:14-16. "Speaking the truth in love" is a key to mature life in Christ. Identify a relationship on your "forgiveness list" (from Exercise 1) where the possibility of resolution requires the courage, grace, and ability to speak the truth in love to one another and to listen. In your journal, squarely face and write out what hurts or bothers you. Charitably consider every possibility that might help you understand the other person's behavior. Note steps you could take to face this matter before it gets worse. In your journal, write what you might say to this person in truth and love.

In prayer, share your thoughts with Christ and listen for a response. Imagine how Jesus might approach the situation. Keep a record of your thoughts and actions.

EXERCISE 3

Read Luke 23:34-43. Dwell on Jesus' prayer of pardon from the cross for those who crucified him (and for one of the thieves crucified with him). We hear and receive in these words the good news of God's pardon for our sin. Extend the circle of grace now by praying these words while keeping before you the names of those you need to forgive. As you pray, consider what Jesus meant by the words, "they do not know what they are doing," when by all appearances on a human level they knew perfectly well. Allow yourself by the grace of the Spirit to enter into the forgiving mind of Christ for those who concern you. Record your learning from inside the mind of Christ.

If you feel ready, write a letter of forgiveness to one of the persons on your debtor list. (See the guidelines on page 80.)

EXERCISE 4

Read Luke 15:11-32. Meditate again on the painting of the Prodigal Son. Consider the costliness of the father's forgiving love. In order to act from his powerful love, the father must first break cultural rules of family relations and religious purity. What advice do you suppose the father received from well-meaning friends or relatives? What might have been the neighbors' reactions to the father's ready reception of his son? Write what you imagine they would have said.

Review your "forgiveness list," reflecting on where you face similar challenges. In what situations could the cost of forgiving affect your image or reputation? What is the likelihood that a third party might view your actions as offensive and irresponsible? Is someone relying on your vengeance to satisfy theirs? Identify the costs and pressures that affect you in your struggle to forgive those on your list. In prayer ask God for the grace and strength to proceed. Dwell on where God is calling you to pass on the gift of forgiveness that God gave you. Note your insights in your journal.

EXERCISE 5

Read Acts 9:10-19. In this story the Lord sends Ananias to lay the hands of Christ's love on Saul, a man infamous for persecuting Christians. Ananias's resistance is rooted in a forgiveness issue: whether or not to risk following the Lord's leading in reaching out with love to an enemy. Ananias, it seems, forgives more for the sake of the Lord than for himself, yet thereby makes way for the unfolding work of God.

What unlikely soul is the Lord prompting you to reach out to, perhaps not so much for your sake as for Christ's? Pray your honest reactions just as Ananias did, and listen for the Lord's guidance. Remember the inexhaustible gift of grace God has bestowed upon you, which God invites you daily to pass on to another. Record your reflections.

Remember to review the insights recorded in your notebook or journal for the week in preparation for the group meeting.

Writing a Letter of Forgiveness

Write a letter of forgiveness to someone toward whom you feel resentment. It could be someone who has already died, or whom you'll never see again. Perhaps it is someone you live or work with. It could be yourself. Who needs forgiveness from you? Write to that person.

First, acknowledge the truth of your negative feelings—all your hurt and anger, your pain and grief. Be absolutely honest.

Then release it. Let go of the burden of your resentment, anger, anguish, and guilt for feeling these things. Confirm that you are doing this in your writing.

Let the matter lie where it will with respect to the other; you cannot be responsible for his or her feelings or responses, only your own. You are choosing to free yourself from this particular bondage to the past.

Remember that God has empowered you to forgive, once and for all, on the Cross. Ask for the grace to let God take the burden from you, now and forever. You may decide at some point to send this letter, or you may not. Regardless, you can expect healing and new energy to flow from this exercise of faith.

Week 7
Seeking Reconciliation

*W*e have not yet resolved many ticklish questions concerning this matter of forgiveness. Does forgiveness mean release from all consequences of sin? Is repentance not a prerequisite? Are there no limits to forgiveness? How do we deal with absent offenders or people who refuse to forgive us? What about justice? We can at least begin to address some of these concerns. As we do so, we will discover some important aspects of the relationship between forgiveness and reconciliation.

Unresolved Questions

We may wonder if forgiveness negates the importance of having to face consequences for wrong behavior. Don't we need certain forms of correction or even punishment to teach us appropriate behavior? This is an interesting question. Children certainly need to learn the connection between act and consequence. They also need to experience forgiveness. Sometimes forgiveness means completely letting go of any consequences we might impose on the offender, while at other times it may not. Again, situations have different characteristics. We may recall from the story of David and Bathsheba that God's forgiveness of David was expressed in sparing his life, but judgment came also in the death of the child born to them. (See 2 Samuel

11–12.) A contemporary story may help to illustrate this dynamic in forgiveness more clearly.

Bishop Donald Tippett was in his office one day when two young men dropped in, hoping to establish an alibi for their planned robbery. When the bishop took a phone call in another room, the young men feared he had sized them up and was about to report them. They attacked him with brass knuckles, doing permanent damage to his left eye. When the two men came to trial, Tippett pleaded for a reduced sentence. He visited them regularly in prison. After the young men were released, the bishop helped one of them financially to further his education and eventually saw him become (of all things!) an ophthalmologist.

Tippett expressed his forgiveness of these men by persevering in returning good for evil. Yet in his realistic love for them, he did not object to their reduced prison sentence. These young men had much to learn; and while learning, they needed to be prevented from doing further harm. They received due punishment under the law even though their victim personally forgave and helped them.

This story corresponds well with one definition of forgiveness suggested in Week 5: *Forgiveness is taking responsibility from my side to release the offender from the alienating effect of the offense on our relationship.* It does not necessarily mean relinquishing all judgment. Discerning between good and evil, wisdom and foolishness, is the legitimate face of human judgment (as opposed to a self-righteous, judgmental attitude). Neither does forgiveness mean releasing the offender from every consequence of the offense. Some consequences we have no control over; some are appropriate for the offender to undergo for the sake of restraint, learning, or justice. But at least from our side, forgiveness breaks the power of the offense to keep us strangers to one another.

Another example of this dynamic would be a situation where the fifteen-year-old daughter comes home one day and says to her parents, "Mom, Dad, I'm pregnant. I just didn't want to say no anymore to my boyfriend." Mom and Dad can sit down and weep with their daughter over her choice and its likely consequences for her young life.

> *Neither is forgiveness a form of absolution.... They must still answer for what they have done, to you, to society, to themselves, to God. This is up to them, not up to you.... Only God gives absolution— and only the sinner can seek it.*
>
> —William A. Meninger

They can forgive her for the pain she is causing them and the hardship she is causing herself. But they cannot undo the fact of her pregnancy. Whatever choice the daughter makes in relation to the child forming within her, she will suffer certain consequences as a result.

What about the relationship between forgiveness and repentance? Some strong arguments place repentance before forgiveness, including many stories and passages in scripture. In the Hebrew scriptures, the consistent theme is that God forgives Israel when the people repent and change their ways. For individual sins too, forgiveness follows repentance. Again, King David had to *acknowledge* his sin against God (by sinning against Uriah the Hittite and his wife Bathsheba) before the prophet Nathan could assure David that God would spare his life.

Humanly speaking, we want those who wrong us to acknowledge their offense and ask for forgiveness. Others will reasonably wish the same of us when we offend or injure them. This is the normal and expected order of things. Psychologically, this order is an important and helpful part of growth toward a forgiving heart. Indeed, many fine thinkers and writers firmly believe that repentance and acts of restitution should always precede forgiveness.[1]

However, both biblical and practical reasons argue that forgiveness can, and often does, proceed without any repentance or restitution. We see this most clearly in scripture at Jesus' crucifixion. Jesus makes an unmistakable statement from the cross that turns the conventional relationship between repentance and forgiveness on its head. He forgives those who torture and murder him before they repent and no doubt with knowledge that many will not do so, even in light of his extraordinary love. This amazing choice is precisely what the apostle Paul marvels over in his letter to the Romans:

> For while we were still weak,...Christ died for the ungodly. Indeed, rarely will anyone die for a *righteous* person....But God proves his love for us in that while we still were sinners Christ died for us. (5:6-8, emphasis added)

God forgives us all, not *because* we are good but before. This does

Our apology puts us "in the way" of forgiveness....I do not mean that our repentance earns forgiveness, either from God or from the injured party.... True forgiveness is possible only as gift, never as payment.
—L. William Countryman

not mean repentance is no longer essential, but that the relationship between it and forgiveness is not quite what we assumed. Forgiveness *does* require repentance, not as a prerequisite but as the only adequate response! God extends a free offer of new life to us—the saving gift of grace—but the meaning and magnitude of the gift require our response, which means turning around and going in God's direction (repentance). If God's forgiveness of us does not result in genuine sorrow for our sin and an effort to live in a way consistent with God's purposes, we clearly have not comprehended the gift nor begun to appropriate it. God then has offered forgiveness, but we have not really received it.

When known and received, forgiveness elicits a response of gratitude. It cannot force any response, of course, but as a gift it begs for response. In the case of offenses that have done dreadful harm, the response to forgiveness may be one of incredulity or stunned awe. The following story from the time of the Turkish genocide in Armenia demonstrates such a response.

> A Turkish officer raided and looted an Armenian home. He killed the aged parents and gave the daughters to the soldiers, keeping the eldest daughter for himself. Some time later she escaped and trained as a nurse. As time passed, she found herself nursing in a ward of Turkish officers. One night, by the light of a lantern, she saw the face of this officer. He was so gravely ill that without exceptional nursing he would die. The days passed, and he recovered. One day, the doctor stood by the bed with her and said to him, "But for her devotion to you, you would be dead." He looked at her and said, "We have met before, haven't we?" "Yes," she said, "we have met before." "Why didn't you kill me?" he asked. She replied, "I am a follower of him who said 'Love your enemies.'"[2]

Try to imagine the impact of this woman's choice upon the officer who had committed such violence against her and her family. He clearly does not comprehend how she could have acted with such extraordinary care for him. In his world, hatred reflexively met hatred. He must have wondered how it was possible for a person to live from such a different center than he knew in himself. But her remarkable expression of genuine care opens a door of possibility to him. Her kindness in response to his brutality exposes his own lack of humanity. It truly heaps "burning coals" of shame upon his head. But if he can bear to face himself honestly, he may find himself walking through the door she has opened and discovering a conversion of life. After all, he too could learn to embody such love. This kind of repentance would be the most fitting response. Here is the hope, the seed of promise, that resides in every act of forgiveness.

Throughout history countless unnamed people have found within themselves the capacity, by faith and grace, to forgive their enemies unilaterally—from their side alone. They bear witness to the power of God in human life. Rather than inducing guilt over our own failures to love and forgive, such stories can stir our imaginations as to what is possible by the gracious power of God's Spirit. What we imagine to be impossible is not so for the God who is making all things new!

> *[Forgiveness] comes to us as a gift, often when we feel least worthy of receiving it.…It can be accepted or rejected. What we do with it is up to us.*
>
> —Johann C. Arnold

Forgiveness and Reconciliation

Following the way of Christ is a serious challenge. As Christians we cannot, in most cases, make another person's repentance a condition of our forgiveness. A culprit's refusal even to acknowledge that a problem exists presents us with a choice. Either we arrest our progress toward forgiveness, or we proceed without the partnership of the offender.

Sometimes in order to stay on the journey we must let go all expectations that the offender will give us the satisfaction of contrition, even after we have forgiven. In this we discover the suffering of forgiveness offered and not received. We can hope and pray that our forgiveness will elicit a penitent heart in response; but if it fails to do so, we must endure the limitations of love offered in freedom. This is a suffering God knows well. Divine grace is exceedingly precious, offered to us at the price of God's own incarnate life in the second person of the Trinity. Yet we can freely choose to reject or ignore the magnitude of God's gift, just as others can freely choose to reject or ignore our gift of forgiveness.

The ultimate aim of forgiveness is reconciliation—restored relationship, the joy of renewed trust and communion. Reconciliation is the final goal, even if we are not emotionally ready for it. Certainly we should not force it if we are not ready. Some may feel that they will never be ready to meet an abuser again this side of the grave. Such feelings are to be respected. But whether in this world or the next, we must eventually come to terms with one another. God's intention is reconciliation for all.

Forgiveness can be unilateral, but reconciliation is by nature a two-way street. It depends on the appropriate response of the other person.

> Reconciliation means full restoration of a whole relationship, and as such requires conscious mutuality. No reconciliation can take place unless the offender recognizes the offense, desires to be forgiven, and is willing to receive forgiveness.[3]

As noted, our forgiveness may remain barren with regard to the hope of reconciliation. If the fruit of forgiveness seems beyond reach despite all our efforts, we must release it as an expectation and hold it as a hope for God's future, in or out of time. While painful because the deeper goal is thwarted, such release frees us to forgive a person who is no longer present on this earth; or a person who will never be seen again and who has no way to know of forgiveness or to respond to it. The persons involved in such situations are sometimes referred to as "absent offenders." I have my own story in this regard.

My father was killed in a train accident when I was eight years old. The train engineer was drunk and allowed the train to speed out of control around a curve. I never knew the engineer. He died in the wreck he caused. As a child, I felt that he certainly deserved to die, that at least some justice had been served. But my anger with him faded. By the time I was a teenager, I realized that alcoholics are deeply unhappy people. I also saw that neither his death nor my feelings would bring back my father, and I ceased bearing any grudge. However, it would be years before I *actively* forgave him. Recently I realized that I'd never done this intentionally and wanted to name my

Saying "I am sorry" is not enough to bring about true reconciliation. The prerequisite to reconciliation is a turning around and a deep change.

—Flora Slosson Wuellner

forgiveness of this stranger. Since he was not present on earth, I went through my process in prayer. Unable to visualize a person I had never met, I focused on the reality of his soul and offered him up to the God who knows and loves him. I told God and this person that I forgave him for his carelessness, for his dishonesty in employment, for the suffering of grief and loss he had caused me all these years.

While this man could not in any tangible way respond, I sensed in my spirit during prayer that a subtle shift had occurred. I felt a deep soul connection and a kind of release that was more complete than before. I sincerely hope this man's soul is free from any residual bondage I might have unconsciously held over him. I pray that his soul may continue to grow and change as it needs to under God's grace. It is important to me that forgiveness free not only me but my offender. After all, God's project in this world is salvation for everyone who can receive it.

As we have already pointed out, our finding the freedom to forgive brings great benefit, quite apart from the satisfaction of repentance or reconciliation. Forgiveness releases us from carrying the weight of judgment in our hearts. It frees us from the corrosive effect of anger and bitterness on our bodies and souls. Yet as persons of faith, our motives for forgiving offenders go beyond self-healing. Forgiveness is not merely therapeutic. A spiritual release accompanies the emotional release, and the spiritual dimension is inherently social.

Sometimes the social dimension of forgiveness is as subtle and unprovable as the inward confirmation of our spirits in prayer. Sometimes the social expression of forgiveness takes the form of an open door, such as the Armenian nurse offered her oppressor first by her actions and then by her words. At times the social dimension of forgiveness comes to full flower as reflected in the story of Bishop Tippett. He actively sought reconciliation with his two attackers, and the benefits eventually became abundantly apparent.

Such stories point us to the sacred ground of forgiveness. Our forgiving is rooted in God's forgiveness of us. Because we know ourselves to be forgiven, we too can forgive. God is in the business of creating a new future out of our mistakes and bad decisions, out of our

Forgiveness is power....It can heal both the forgiver and the forgiven. In fact, it could change the world if we allowed it to.

—Johann C. Arnold

wounds and our woundings. The Holy One is interested in healing the past and helping us move into the reality of God's own realm, called in scripture "the kingdom of God." Are we willing to join the great divine plan of creating a new future? We can do so if we are more interested in redemption than revenge.

Redeeming those in captivity, recovering what is lost, turning curses to blessings, finding cause for hope where there seems to be none, bringing life out of death—this is the central stuff of Christian faith. Next week we will look more closely at the social implications of forgiveness and the concept of justice best suited to it. Finally we will return to the idea of the blessed life with which we began.

Only a free person can live with an uneven score.

—Lewis B. Smedes

DAILY EXERCISES

When you have read Week 7, "Seeking Reconciliation," be sure to note reflections, questions, and images in your journal. This week's exercises give you an opportunity to reflect further on the relationship between forgiveness and reconciliation from the posture both of the offender and the offended. They will also suggest ways to pray in situations where direct personal reconciliation is not or may not be possible in this world. As you engage the exercises this week, begin to think about what forgiveness and reconciliation might look like in your own household, neighborhood, work setting, or congregation. Remember to keep gathering stories of forgiveness and reconciliation, and take these stories with you to the weekly meeting.

EXERCISE 1

Read Luke 15:25-32. Meditate on the art of the Prodigal Son. Jesus seems to have left it to his listeners to complete the parable of the Prodigal Son. The younger son was lost and is found, but what about the elder son? In what sense is the elder son not truly "at home" yet? What would it take for him to let himself "be found" as well? What will he do with his anger? Reflect on how you would finish the story. You might want to write a dialogue between the elder son and the father, or between the two brothers. You might draw a picture of how you see the ending.

    Now return to your own reality. Return to your "forgiveness list." Recall where you have hard feelings toward someone, perhaps in your own family, that you have carried inside you for too long. How would you finish your own story? What has to happen before change can occur? Pray to God for the desire and courage you need to do your part. Pray for the other person as well, with the inner eye of love.

EXERCISE 2

Read Genesis 32:3-21. The backdrop to this story is Jacob's deceit against his brother, first in tricking Esau out of his birthright (25:29-34) and later stealing his father's blessing (chapter 27). Jacob is deeply

afraid of meeting his brother against whom he sinned so many years earlier. He creates several layers of gifts between himself and the dreaded confrontation with his brother, hoping to soften what he presumes is still Esau's resentful heart.

Reflect on how you typically approach a person you know you have offended or wronged. Have you ever tried, like Jacob, to appease the offended party or "make nice" without actually owning up to what you did or stating that you were sorry? The most helpful approach in such situations is not appeasement but apology. Identify someone you need to apologize to and write a clean, straightforward apology (guidelines on page 92). You may choose to send it in writing or to let this practice inform a verbal apology. Pray for the humility and courage to act when you are ready.

Exercise 3

Read Matthew 18:10-20. In this passage Jesus gives us, the church, a discipline for seeking reconciliation with those who sin against us. Review the different levels of action that Jesus proposes for seeking restoration of relationships. How does this process compare to the way your church usually deals with injured relationships? How does your church encourage and guide reconciliation among people?

Think of someone in the church who has sinned against you. In what ways is the other person (or you) like a "lost sheep" who needs to be found? Imagine approaching your offender one-on-one in such a spirit, speaking the truth in love. What would you say, and what do you feel could happen? If the other person refused your appeal, whom could you ask to help in a creative and redemptive way? If the person still refused your efforts to restore the peace, what would it mean to treat him or her the way Jesus treated Gentiles and tax collectors? Spend a few minutes reflecting on your responsibility in this situation. Pray for the other person and your openness to grace and truth.

Exercise 4

Read Matthew 5:21-26. Pay particular attention to verses 23-24, noting that Jesus' concern is with those who may have something against us, not those we have something against. Make a list of all those persons you know or suspect have a grievance against you, whether based in fact or perception of what you did or failed to do. Reflect in complete honesty on what it will mean to "be reconciled" in these situations and what initiative of responsibility or love on your part might bridge the gulf. Think in terms of first steps: Is a candid conversation needed to clarify your mutual understanding of what happened? Is an apology called for? Does your sorrow or repentance need to be shown in an act of contrition or meaningful restitution?

Lift in prayer each person you have listed, earnestly desiring his or her spiritual well-being. Give to God any defensiveness or pride that could block the expression of your own love. Record thoughts and feelings in your journal.

EXERCISE 5

Read Ephesians 4:30-5:2. The anger we hold in our hearts grieves the Holy Spirit, whose tenderheartedness we are urged to imitate as beloved children of God. We are asked to forgive "one another, as God in Christ has forgiven [us]." In so doing we participate in the fragrant offering of Christ's sacrificial love. Sometimes we hold onto bitterness because there is no person alive or within our reach whom we can actively reconcile with. Yet because our souls are interconnected in God, the opportunity is not lost.

Identify someone, dead or alive, with whom you desire reconciliation and who seems impossible to contact personally. Take this person with you into prayer, asking God to enfold you both in light and peace. Ask for or offer forgiveness in the depths of your spirit and ask Christ to mediate between you. Pray for the spiritual freedom of the other person and for your own inner release from guilt or anger. Pay close attention to your feelings and intuition in prayer. Offer thanks for whatever gift of spiritual healing you may sense has occurred and for the hope of full reconciliation in God's own future.

Remember to review the insights recorded in your notebook or journal for the week in preparation for the group meeting.

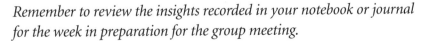

Guidelines for Writing a Good Apology

1. *Be respectful of the person you are writing to. Courtesy and tact are important.*

2. *Do not try to defend yourself, make excuses, or explain all the circumstances from your perspective.*

3. *Go right to the point and use simple, direct language.*

Following these basic principles will result in a "clean, straightforward apology." It is a genuine spiritual discipline to exercise these guidelines consistently.

Week 8
Becoming the
Beloved Community

This week we want to consider further the impact of forgiveness and reconciliation on society as a whole. We will reflect on a different way of understanding justice within the framework of forgiveness. Finally we will connect these perspectives to the Beatitudes that started us on this journey eight weeks ago.

Forgiveness in the Social Order

It is most important to see that forgiveness and reconciliation affect more than our personal relationships. When many people of faith commit to living from a basic stance of love and hope, when even small communities persevere in cultivating forgiveness in the face of injustice and oppression, whole societies can change.

We have some remarkable evidence of this truth from the past century. Within the United States, the principles of the civil rights movement included loving and praying for the enemy. Martin Luther King Jr. took his cues from Jesus' teachings and from the effectiveness of Gandhi's nonviolent resistance to the British in India a few decades earlier. King accurately saw a kind of spiritual pragmatism in Jesus' command to love our enemies. Instead of an impossible ideal, he perceived it as a powerful tool for political as well as personal change. Here is what he wrote in his book *Strength to Love*:

It is not enough to weep silently over the losses sustained in child abuse, divorce, AIDS, torture, health care for the indigent elderly, and violence that divide families and nations. It is also important to draw these collisions among persons, positions, and within systems to everyone's attention.

—Doris Donnelly

Far from being the pious injunction of a Utopian dreamer, the command to love one's enemies is an absolute necessity for our survival. Love even for enemies is the key to the solution of the problems of our world....

...Darkness cannot drive out darkness; only light can do that. Hate cannot drive out hate; only love can do that....

...Love is the only force capable of transforming an enemy into a friend. We never get rid of an enemy by meeting hate with hate; we get rid of an enemy by getting rid of enmity....Love transforms with redemptive power.[1]

> *Love is the only power that can overcome evil without using evil means.*
>
> —John S. Mogabgab

King viewed love as a spiritual-political weapon in a world where black and white Americans would be living together for years to come. He understood that forgiveness could bring about a level of lasting change unattainable by other means. He wrote passionately about developing and maintaining the capacity to forgive:

It is impossible even to begin the act of loving one's enemies without the prior acceptance of the necessity, over and over again, of forgiving those who inflict evil and injury upon us....

Forgiveness does not mean ignoring what has been done or putting a false label on an evil act. It means...that the evil act no longer remains as a barrier to the relationship. Forgiveness is a catalyst creating the atmosphere necessary for a fresh start and a new beginning....

To our most bitter opponents we say: "We shall match your capacity to inflict suffering by our capacity to endure suffering. We shall meet your physical force with soul force. Do to us what you will, and we shall continue to love you. We cannot in all good conscience obey your unjust laws, because non-co-operation with evil is as much a moral obligation as is co-operation with good....But...we will wear you down by our capacity to suffer. One day we shall win freedom, but not only for ourselves. We shall so appeal to your heart and conscience that we shall win *you* in the process, and our victory will be a double victory."[2]

Martin Luther King Jr. held in his heart the vision of a just, peaceful, and integrated globe. He called this world the Beloved Community. It was a hope for the future but equally an imperative call for the present. The power of this vision fed the preaching and action through which he held up its beauty to others. More than any single African American, King's leadership set the stage for the crumbling of segregation laws in the South and the extension of basic civil rights to American citizens of all races. Like the British who could not continue to fire on row after row of Indian salt mine workers protesting nonviolently, white Americans could not bear to watch night after night on television the violence of the powerful against the nonviolence of the unarmed. The justice of the black person's cause was all the more apparent by virtue of the tactics used. If protests had been violent, they would have given those in power more fuel for an ideology of repression. The witness of the civil rights movement did not convert everyone, but a majority of the nation was indeed won over.

We need to note several points of great significance in King's words above. First, he calls evil evil. He understands that forgiveness has the power to undo evil, not in the sense of changing what is past but in the sense of changing future possibilities. Second, because forgiveness is oriented toward a new future, King desires to win the friendship of those who are now enemies. He wants reconciliation, not mere victory of his people's cause over and against the others. Third, he makes it clear that this approach does not cooperate with injustice. The love of his followers for their enemies does not depend on the enemies' justice, but neither will it abide by the enemies' unjust laws.

Forgiveness and Justice

This brings us to the matter of justice in relation to forgiveness. Many people believe that forgiveness and justice are opposed responses, as if opting for one erases the other. "How can I forgive? I want to see justice done." It seems to them that forgiveness mocks the claims of justice or gives wrongdoers a dispensation from accountability.

One particular and somewhat narrow view of justice is essentially punishment or retaliation, a way of "evening out the score." Called "retributive justice," it serves as a foundation of our legal system. We would generally expect a court of law to operate on this concept of justice, and such justice holds an important place in society.

But for those whose faith is rooted in the Bible, justice means something far bigger and more significant. The prophet Micah touches on it with his famous question, "What does the Lord require of you but to do justice, and to love kindness, and to walk humbly with your God?" (6:8) Micah sketches, in a few brush strokes, the essential elements of the right way of human life. To do justice in biblical times meant basically to do right by one another—to honor family and neighbor according to the commandments, to share resources fairly and generously, to care for the weaker ones among them (aging parents, widows, orphans). Justice bore a close relationship to kindness, humility, and faithfulness. So justice is a way of living together that makes for *shalom*, peace that is not merely the absence of conflict but the rich wholeness of a community whose members live in mutual respect, freedom, and joy. Not surprisingly, the biblical understanding of *shalom* strongly resembles Martin Luther King's vision of the Beloved Community, although King translates it into the global, multicultural reality of our modern world.

Forgiveness makes perfect sense in the context of the biblical concept of justice. Forgiveness is one of the best ways to form *shalom* in human community. It looks to a future where we can live together more justly, instead of merely trying to even the score of the past. In this way, forgiveness provides an excellent foundation for justice. The goal is to restore human beings to all they can be by God's grace and to restore human community beyond the wounds of the past toward the future God is creating for us (and with us if we are willing to join the divine purpose). This understanding has been called "restorative justice."

In his book *No Future without Forgiveness*, Bishop Desmond Tutu writes poignantly of his experience with the Truth and Reconciliation Commission of South Africa. The commission's aim was not criminal investigation but the creation of a place where truth-telling could occur on both sides of the apartheid struggle with limited amnesty granted to those who pleaded guilty to violence. The hearings allowed confession, forgiveness, and healing to begin in a safe environment. What had happened in secret under apartheid began

Keep struggling against hatred and resentment. At times you will have the upper hand, at times you will feel beaten down....Never stop trying to live the commandment of love and forgiveness. Do not dilute the strength of Jesus's message;...do not dismiss it as unreal and impractical. Do not cut it to your size....Keep it as it is, aspire to it, desire it, and work for its achievement.

—Naim Ateek

to come to light before the nation where it could be recognized for what it was, with all the accompanying feelings of revulsion, sorrow, amazement, and inspiration. The process of truth-telling gradually led a whole nation through its dark, divisive past into a place where moving forward together as equal citizens might begin. Writing of the noble side of the human spirit under oppression, Tutu marvels:

> It is quite incredible the capacity people have shown to be magnanimous—refusing to be consumed by bitterness and hatred, willing to meet with those who have violated their persons and their rights, willing to meet in a spirit of forgiveness and reconciliation, eager only to know the truth, to know the perpetrator so that they could forgive them.…
>
> …We have survived the ordeal and we are realizing that we can indeed transcend the conflicts of the past, we can hold hands as we realize our common humanity.[3]

There is a hard law.… When an injury is done to us, we never recover until we forgive.

—Alan Paton

The Truth and Reconciliation Commission of South Africa existed for the primary purpose of serving not retributive but restorative justice. Like God's justice, the aim was redemptive. Churches in the United States have expressed renewed interest in this idea; "restorative justice" is becoming something of a movement. Already the concept is making inroads in our justice system. People may receive training in the principles of restorative justice, which attempts to bring together offenders, offended, and their communities for the healing of all concerned. As understanding grows, apology, restitution, forgiveness, and reconciliation become possible.

When we think about forgiveness in relation to justice, a simple truth may help detach us from the draw of retributive justice. The truth is this: We cannot make the past right. No amount of punishment or restitution can compensate for the damage done by certain acts. Retaliation only feeds the cycle of anger and hatred. Even those who fiercely desired the execution of their loved one's murderers have often not found through such "justice" any deep sense of peace or closure. Their bitterness sometimes continues as they wish the execution could have been more painful or they fantasize about the tortures of hell for the murderer's soul. They do not perceive that they torture themselves with a living hell by holding onto their hatred and rage, by feeding their pain, and by reliving in imagination the suffering of their loved one.

Only forgiveness can bring such persons to a new place—a place of inner peace, freedom, and true closure. Forgiveness has this power. It is God's gift to us for the healing of the nations. Forgiveness offers the power of love to release and transform us, to breathe the fresh air of life into stale prisons of pain in continual replay.

Forgiving does not require us to forget but to remember without rancor. To remember well is to hold both the victim and the victimizer in God's grace, with prayer for every form of healing and blessing for both. God's project in the world is to redeem all, heal all, bless all. When the gift of forgiveness has freed us from our desire to condemn and punish the guilty one, we need not assume that all evidence of our wound will be gone. The risen Christ still bore on his body the marks of his crucifixion. But his scars were transfigured into signs of his victory over sin and death and have become for us a promise of participation in Jesus' victory as well.

> *God wants to show that there is life after conflict and repression—that because of forgiveness there is a future.*
>
> —Desmond M. Tutu

The scars of our wounds will always be with us. But they can be taken up into God's larger purposes of new life and transformed into signs of promise, if we willingly allow God to fill our wounds with the love of Christ. God can take our pain and bring something good from it, no matter how horrific or traumatic the circumstances. Our life experience is not unlike compost. If we allow it to be aerated by grace, if we are patient with the conditions of each day, in time it will become the rich soil of new life. God is always working for good for those who love God.

The Life of Blessing

Now we return to the blessing. Maybe the life of blessedness Jesus describes in the Beatitudes is not so crazy after all. It is not the wisdom of the world; it is the wisdom of God. The Beatitudes describe the kind of people who are best suited to the kingdom of God, for the realm of heaven is unalterably marked by love. Forgiveness, one of the chief expressions of God's love for us, is meant to be a habit of heart in our love for one another. When we know with deep certainty that we have been blessed by divine mercy and goodness, we have the strength to share that blessing.

In the final analysis, forgiveness can only emerge from great strength of soul. It is a clear sign of the courageous, humble resilience of the human spirit undergirded by grace. Forgiveness says yes to life, hope, the future. It holds out the possibility of redemption for the offender and the offended, joining in God's fond project for this world. What a blessed state of mind and heart it is to be free to forgive. What a blessed experience it is to receive forgiveness from another. Can we allow ourselves to be so generously loved by God that we in turn can love others that much? Can we become, by grace, the Beloved Community? This is the privilege, the joy, the wonder held open to us. May we be willing to receive and share the bounty!

This is how the gospel, the good news, eventually delivers us from an unforgiving spirit. It doesn't work by admonishing us....It works by overwhelming us with love, by drawing us toward the One who loves us....It drives out hurt and anger by means of pleasure, joy, delight, love, life.
—L. William Countryman

DAILY EXERCISES

Read Week 8, "Becoming the Beloved Community." Note your questions and insights in the margins of the Participant's Book or in your journal.

In 2 Corinthians 5:17, the Apostle Paul writes that "in Christ, there is a new creation: everything old has passed away; see, everything has become new!" This week's daily exercises challenge us to listen for how Christ calls us to participate in the new thing God is doing to restore the human family. The question is, How do we pattern our lives, personally and corporately, so that God's blessing is known and shared? Keep your eyes and ears open for stories showing forgiveness and reconciliation. Take them to the group session.

EXERCISE 1

Read Matthew 5:43-48. Now reread the words of Martin Luther King Jr. on page 94. Underline the phrases that convey to you the real power and challenge in Jesus' teaching to "love your enemies and pray for those who persecute you. Reflect on those phrases. How and where do they challenge you to rise to the call? Complete your time by soaking in the steadfast love of God for a few minutes. Pray for those who require of you "soul force" and note any thoughts in your journal.

EXERCISE 2

Read Luke 14:12-14. In this story Jesus gives instructions to his host concerning whom to invite to future parties: those he would not normally include, those least capable of returning the favor, those most in need fellowship, etc. Plan a party or social gathering based on Jesus' instructions in this passage. Draw up an invitation list, being as specific as you can about persons. Then reflect on your thought process. Whom would you have the hardest time inviting? Who would have the hardest time accepting? Who would be most surprised or honored by your invitation?

Now take your list to the Lord in prayer. Pray for each person in turn. Ask the Spirit to guide your next steps.

EXERCISE 3

Read Colossians 3:12-17. Ponder these powerful words that Paul addressed to an early Christian community struggling with divisive issues. What divisive issues in your church community (local, denominational, or ecumenical) would Paul address with words like these? What do Paul's words suggest about how we remain united in Christ even in our differences?

Prayerfully dwell on each word and phrase while keeping in mind your own church community, especially those who differ with you on certain issues. Listen for where Christ is calling you to "put on" new clothing or practice something new. Record what you hear.

EXERCISE 4

Read Ephesians 2:11-22. In this passage Paul speaks of Christ making "both groups into one" and breaking down "the dividing wall" (v.14). As you reread the passage, consider what "dividing walls" Christ would break down in your community.

Draw a "reconciliation map" of your local community by sketching a visual image of the walls that partition the landscape of your community and its relationships. Ponder how the Christ who broke down walls between Gentiles and Jews might bring peace to your community as well. Pray that the walls might fall. Listen for where Christ is asking you to confess your sin or to forgive the sin of another. Listen for where Christ is calling you to greater justice.

EXERCISE 5

Read Romans 8:18-25. Paul tells us that the whole world waits with eager longing for the revealing of the children of God. Where do you see creation "subjected to futility" and the "bondage of decay"? How do you participate in these realities?

Note down the qualities of the "children of God" that all creation longs for and that the world desperately needs in order to be reborn in hope. Which of these qualities do you see emerging in yourself? In prayer, make yourself available to be the person God wants and needs you to be for the sake of the world.

An Annotated Resource List
from Upper Room Ministries

*T*he following books relate to and expand on the subject matter of the eight weeks of *Companions in Christ: The Way of Forgiveness.* As you read and share with your small group, you may find some material that particularly challenges or helps you. If you wish to pursue individual reading on your own or if your small group wishes to follow up with additional resources, this list may be useful. The Upper Room is the publisher of all of the books listed, and the number in parentheses is the product number to give when ordering.

An Adventure in Healing and Wholeness: The Healing Ministry of Christ in the Church Today (0-8358-0689-8) by James K. Wagner condenses Wagner's successful workshop on healing and wholeness into an easy-to-use workbook format. Field-tested and designed for church groups, this seven-session study explains the holistic approach to health and the relationship between prayer and healing. It also offers individual and group reflection, study materials, and information needed to begin a healing ministry within a congregation.

An Adventure in Healing and Wholeness: The Healing Ministry of Christ in the Church Today (Korean translation) (0-8358-0840-8) by James K. Wagner, translated by Daniel Y. Shin, brings Wagner's successful workbook on healing and wholeness to Korean Christians and churches. The workbook adapts Wagner's popular workshop into a seven-session format that explores a holistic approach to health and the relationship between prayer and healing. *An Adventure in Healing and Wholeness* offers individual and group reflection, study materials, and information needed to begin a healing ministry within a congregation.

Una Aventura en Sanidad y Plenitud: El Ministerio de Sanidad de Cristo en la Iglesia de Hoy (Spanish translation) (0-8358-0773-8) by James K. Wagner.

Anchoring Your Well Being: Christian Wholeness in a Fractured World (0-8358-0821-1) by Howard Clinebell offers suggestions for leading a healthier life in seven dimensions: spiritually, physically, mentally, in relationships, in work and play, environmentally, and in crisis and loss. Biblical texts provide guidance and a basis for holistic health, as Clinebell reminds us that God's desire for all the earth remains a vision of wholeness and health. A guide for congregational leaders or group study is available.

Anchoring Your Well Being: Christian Wholeness in a Fractured World, A Guide for Congregational Leaders (0-8358-0822-X) by Howard Clinebell helps congregational leaders develop wellness programs in their churches. Such programs can become one of the most reward-ing and appreciated parts of a congregation's overall ministry, Clinebell says. To be used with *Anchoring Your Well Being*, this guide offers back-ground information, ideas to implement wellness, and tailored study sessions for different groups.

Breaking and Mending: Divorce and God's Grace (0-8358-0855-6) by Mary Lou Redding weaves her personal story with those from scrip-ture to help other Christians who are facing divorce find God's grace in the midst of pain. *Breaking and Mending* looks at the spiritual issues of divorce, rather than the sociological ones, and allows the scriptures to illuminate and heal those who face this difficult tran-sition. Chapters deal with forgiveness, breaking old patterns, broken dreams, and healing.

Discovering Grace in Grief (0-8358-0696-0) by James L. Mayfield is a personal book written for those who are grieving—primarily the death of a loved one. James L. Mayfield takes us through the various stages of grief, offering insights from the Christian faith that will com-fort and sustain all who grieve.

Feed My Shepherds: Spiritual Healing and Renewal for Those in Christian Leadership (0-8358-0845-9) by Flora Slosson Wuellner examines the issues related to burnout. Jesus said, "Feed my sheep." Yet those who engage in feeding others need to be nourished themselves. In a powerful and welcome new book, one of our most popular authors looks at the shepherd's need to be spiritually fed, giving much needed focus to the struggles and burnout of those in caregiving ministries. Wuellner uses the healing relationship between the risen Jesus and his disciples as a model for the inner healing and renewal of today's Christian leaders, both lay and clergy. Drawing on scriptures from the Gospels' post-Resurrection narratives, Wuellner adds spiritual reflection, personal questions, and guided meditations to address a variety of needs.

Forgiveness, the Passionate Journey: Nine Steps of Forgiving through Jesus' Beatitudes (0-8358-0945-5) by Flora Slosson Wuellner looks at the difficulties of forgiving. Why are we so often told we should forgive, but so seldom shown the steps by which forgiveness is possible? Wuellner explores the Beatitudes to see the deeper meanings of forgiveness. She helps us recognize new ways of relating to one another within the vision offered by Jesus in the nine Beatitudes from the Sermon on the Mount. In these blessings we discover an open door to new, healed ways of relating to God, to others, to ourselves, to the communities around us, and to generations behind us. Wuellner helps us to see how we have misunderstood the radical depths of Christ's New Creation of reconciliation.

Inner Healing for Broken Vessels: Seven Steps to a Woman's Way of Healing (0-8358-0670-7) by Linda H. Hollies offers seven steps to healing from painful experiences: recognition, admission, sharing, confession, reconciliation, choosing to be different, and daily choices. Each chapter weaves together struggles of contemporary women with those of women in biblical times. This personal book will serve as a woman's lifeline to renewal, healing, and spiritual direction.

Prayer and Our Bodies (0-8358-0568-9) by Flora Slosson Wuellner invites us into a new relationship with our bodies. In guiding us to pray both for and with our bodies, she introduces a greater awareness of the interaction between body, mind, and spirit. Using prayer and guided meditations centered on the healing Christ of scripture, Wuellner explores how the body can identify inner stresses and hurts.

Prayer, Stress, and Our Inner Wounds (0-8358-0501-8) by Flora Slosson Wuellner describes several types of pain—physical pain, painful memories, forgotten wounds, the pain of uncertainty, and the pain of stress and anxiety—and reminds us that the passion to heal was central in Jesus' ministry. God's grace moves through this caring book to work in the lives of readers as they confront their own needs and pains.

Release: Healing from Wounds of Family, Church, and Community (0-8358-0775-4) by Flora Slosson Wuellner addresses the emotional burdens and psychic wounds we inherit from our communities. Guiding us into a new frontier of healing, she explores the signs and symptoms of communal bondage and burdens. Designed for individual and group use, her book features guided meditations and healing prayers for whole communities, including families, churches, coworkers, and gender or ethnic groups.

The Spiritual Formation Bible: Growing in Intimacy with God through Scripture invites you to enter into the biblical message with vitality and freshness, as it encourages you to dig deep and read reflectively. By providing simple, attractive, and practical ways to listen for God's word, *The Spiritual Formation Bible* helps you connect your own life stories with the great story of God's redemptive activity in history. Special features encourage spiritual growth: Getting Started articles provide wisdom on various aspects of spiritual formation. Book introductions point to important themes of each book of the Bible. Entry Points take a passage of Scripture and explore themes of special importance for spiritual growth. Ways of Meeting God articles tie Entry Points to practical ways you can grow spiritually. Glimpses from the Classics are brief excerpts from some of the wisest and most profound writings on the spiritual life. Indexes help you find topics of special relevance to spiritual formation. Available in two translations and three bindings.

0-310-90211-8	Paperback NIV
0-310-90210-X	Hardcover NIV
0-310-90089-1	Hardcover NRSV
0-310-90212-6	Leather NIV
0-310-90090-5	Leather NRSV

The Spiritual Heart of Your Health: A Devotional Guide on the Healing Stories of Jesus (0-8358-0958-7) by James K. Wagner teaches us that Jesus helped each person he met to be whole and healthy in body, mind, spirit, and healthy in relationships. Wagner looks at thirty healing encounters with Jesus from the Gospels. More than offering a Bible study, James Wagner teaches us a process to pray for healing as we read and study these passages. Basing his work on the *lectio divina* tradition of praying the scriptures, Wagner begins each meditation with a prayer. He includes the text of scripture (usually from the Contemporary English Version), a short explanation of the passage, a brief quotation from church tradition, and questions for personal reflection. Written in a workbook format to record insights and answers, this book may be used by individuals or small groups.

Stretch Out Your Hand: Exploring Healing Prayer (0-8358-0872-6) by Tilda Norberg and Robert D. Webber suggests that healing is not just getting well from an illness but a beautiful dynamic process leading to the wholeness that God wills for us. This book addresses tough questions such as: "Why isn't everyone who prays healed?" and "What is the role of faith in healing?" Through their candid writing style, the authors offer practical ways for us to consider the varieties of God's healing love for individuals, institutions, and communities. *Stretch Out Your Hand* provides an honest examination of the many difficult questions about prayer and the role of faith in healing.

Stretch Out Your Hand: Exploring Healing Prayer, a *Leader's Guide* (0-8358-0871-8) by Tilda Norberg and Robert D. Webber provides

the structure, insights and suggestions to lead a six-week, small-group study using the book *Stretch Out Your Hand*.

When the World Breaks Your Heart: Spiritual Ways of Living with Tragedy (0-8358-0842-4) by Gregory S. Clapper teaches us how to survive tragedy. When United Airlines Flight 232 crashed in Sioux City, Iowa, 113 people died while 183 survived. Clapper, a National Guard chaplain, ministered to the survivors at the scene, to the families of those who died and later to others in the community, and to the National Guard Unit members who assisted in the rescue. Using stories from this experience, Clapper offers hope for living with tragedies that inevitably come to us all and helps us see God's presence in the midst of these times.

The Workbook on Lessons from the Saints (0-8358-0965-X) by Maxie Dunnam helps us gain spiritual insight through the reading and interpretation of the writings of those generations that have gone before us, the saints. In this eight-week, small-group study, Dr. Dunnam suggests how Christians today can find spiritual growth by imitating the lives of earlier generations of Christians. Dunnam examines the lives and writings of saints such as Martin Luther, John Wesley, Francis de Sales, Margery Kempe, Jean-Pierre de Caussade, François Fénelon, and Thérèse of Lisieux.

Notes

Week 1: Living in God's Blessing

1. *The Collected Works of St. Teresa of Avila*, vol. 2, trans. Kieran Kavanaugh and Otilio Rodriguez (Washington, D.C.: ICS Publications, 1980), 283–84.

2. John Claypool, *Mending the Heart* (Cambridge, Mass.: Cowley Publications, 1999), 12.

Week 2: Releasing Shame and Guilt

1. Roberta C. Bondi, "Out of the Green-Tiled Bathroom: Crucifixion," *Weavings* 9, no. 5 (September/October 1994): 8, 10.

2. Ibid., 11.

3. Ibid., 26.

4. Sister Helen Prejean, *Dead Man Walking: An Eyewitness Account of the Death Penalty in the United States* (New York: Vintage Books, 1994), 82.

5. Ibid., 162.

Week 4: Transforming Anger

1. John S. Mogabgab, "Editor's Introduction," *Weavings* 9, no. 2 (March/April 1994): 2.

2. Adele J. Gonzales, "Finding God in Your Anger," *Weavings* 9, no. 2 (March/April 1994): 42.

3. From Judith E. Smith's review of Andrew D. Lester's book, *Coping with Your Anger: A Christian Guide,* in *Weavings* 9, no. 2 (March/April 1994): 46.

4. Mogabgab, "Editor's Introduction," 3.

5. C. Gordon Peerman III, "Anger: An Instrument of Peace," *Weavings* 9, no. 2 (March/April 1994): 17.

6. E. Glenn Hinson, "On Coping with Your Anger," *Weavings* 9, no. 2 (March/April 1994): 34.

7. Wendy Wright, in a presentation to the Pathways-Weavings Retreat, 11 October 2001.

8. Madeleine L'Engle, *The Weather of the Heart: Poems by Madeleine L'Engle* (Wheaton, Ill.: Harold Shaw Publishers, 1978), 84.

9. Hinson, "On Coping with Your Anger," 39.

10. Ibid., 36.

11. Robert C. Morris, "The Second Breath: Frustration As a Doorway to Daily Spiritual Practice," *Weavings* 13, no. 2 (March/April 1998): 43–44.

WEEK 5: RECEIVING GOD'S FORGIVENESS

1. Anthony Bloom, *Living Prayer* (Springfield, Ill.: Templegate Publishers, 1966), 31.

2. Christopher D. Marshall, *Beyond Retribution: A New Testament Vision for Justice, Crime, and Punishment* (Grand Rapids, Mich.: William B. Eerdmans Publishing Co., 2001), 264.

3. Marjorie J. Thompson, "Moving Toward Forgiveness," *Weavings* 7, no. 2 (March/April 1992): 19.

4. Marjorie J. Thompson's updated definition, articulated in a T. V. Moore Lecture entitled "Releasing the Captive: Forgiveness as Participation in God's Compassion," given at San Francisco Theological Seminary 4 April 1997.

5. L. Gregory Jones, *Embodying Forgiveness: A Theological Analysis* (Grand Rapids, Mich.: William B. Eerdmans Publishing Co., 1995), 228–29.

6. L. William Countryman, *Forgiven and Forgiving* (Harrisburg, Pa.: Morehouse Publishing, 1998), 63.

7. Jones, *Embodying Forgiveness*, 15.

8. Ibid., 5.

9. Douglas V. Steere, *Dimensions of Prayer: Cultivating a Relationship with God*, rev. ed. (Nashville, Tenn.: Upper Room Books, 2002), 45–46.

10. Countryman, *Forgiven and Forgiving*, 24.

WEEK 6: FORGIVING OTHERS

1. Thomas Merton, trans., *The Wisdom of the Desert: Sayings from the Desert Fathers of the Fourth Century* (New York: New Directions Publishing, 1960), 75–76.

2. Wendy Wright, "Finding God in Family Life," *Praying* 21(November/December 1987): 8.

3. Carol Luebering, *The Forgiving Family: First Steps to Reconciliation* (Cincinnati, Ohio: St. Anthony Messenger Press, 1983), 57–58.

4. Robert Muller, quoted in "Decide to Forgive," from the syndicated newspaper column "Dear Abby," 16 January 1989.

5. Lance Morrow, "I Spoke As a Brother," *Time* (9 January 1984): 33.

WEEK 7: SEEKING RECONCILIATION

1. See, for example, Marie M. Fortune, "Forgiveness: The Last Step," in Anne L. Horton and Judith A. Williamson, ed., *Abuse and Religion: When Praying Isn't Enough* (New York: Macmillan, 1988), 215–20. Marie Fortune has played a key role in bringing to public and church attention serious issues in family violence and sexual abuse. Her view of forgiveness is primarily therapeutic and psychological rather than theological.

2. Geoffrey Wainwright, *Doxology: The Praise of God in Worship, Doctrine, and Life* (New York: Oxford University Press, 1980), 434.

3. Thompson, "Moving Toward Forgiveness," 21.

WEEK 8: BECOMING THE BELOVED COMMUNITY

1. Martin Luther King Jr., *Strength to Love* (Phildelphia, Pa.: Fortress Press, 1981), 47–48, 51, 52.

2. Ibid., 48, 55, 54–55.

3. Desmond Mpilo Tutu, *No Future without Forgiveness* (New York: Doubleday, 1999), 120.

Sources and Authors
of Marginal Quotations

WEEK 1: LIVING IN GOD'S BLESSING

Roberta C. Bondi, "Becoming Bearers of Reconciliation," *Weavings* 5, no. 1 (January/February 1990): 7.

Desmond M. Tutu, "Allies of God,", *Weavings* 5, no. 1(January/February 1990): 39.

Flora Slosson Wuellner, *Forgiveness, the Passionate Journey: Nine Steps of Forgiving through Jesus' Beatitudes* (Nashville, Tenn.: Upper Room Books, 2001), 53.

WEEK 2: RELEASING SHAME AND GUILT

Henri J. M. Nouwen, "Forgiveness: The Name of Love in a Wounded World," *Weavings* 7, no. 2 (March/April 1992): 11.

William Moremen, review of *Is Human Forgiveness Possible? A Pastoral Care Perspective*, by John Patton, *Weavings* 7, no. 2 (March/April 1992): 42

George Hunsinger, "Jesus and the Leper," *Weavings* 5, no. 1 (January/February 1990): 34.

Wuellner, *Forgiveness,* 22.

L. William Countryman, *Forgiven and Forgiving* (Harrisburg, Pa.: Morehouse Publishing, 1998), 55–56.

WEEK 3: FACING OUR ANGER

Sandra M. Flaherty, *Woman, Why Do You Weep? Spirituality for Survivors of Childhood Sexual Abuse* (New York: Paulist Press, 1992), 140.

L. Gregory Jones, *Embodying Forgiveness: A Theological Analysis* (Grand Rapids, Mich.: William B. Eerdmans Publishing Co., 1995), 242.

Wuellner, *Forgiveness,* 36.

WEEK 4: TRANSFORMING ANGER

Dennis Linn, Sheila Fabricant Linn, and Matthew Linn, *Don't Forgive Too Soon* (New York: Paulist Press, 1997), 42.

Jane E. Vennard, *Praying for Friends and Enemies: Intercessory Prayer* (Minneapolis, Minn.: Augsburg Fortress Publishers, 1995), 41.

William A. Meninger, *The Process of Forgiveness* (New York: Continuum, 1996), 22.

Vennard, *Praying for Friends and Enemies,* 39.

WEEK 5: RECEIVING GOD'S FORGIVENESS

Johann Cristoph Arnold, *Why Forgive?* (Farmington, Pa.: The Plough Publishing House, 2000), 1.

C. Gordon Peerman III, "Discovering Forgiveness," *Weavings* 7, no. 2 (March/April 1992): 39.

Wuellner, *Forgiveness,* 73–75.

Countryman, *Forgiven and Forgiving,* 78.

Ibid., 92.

WEEK 6: FORGIVING OTHERS

Nouwen, "Forgiveness," 15.

Walter Wink, *Engaging the Powers: Discernment and Resistance in a World of Domination* (Minneapolis, Minn.: Augsburg Fortress, 1992), 176.

Linn, *Don't Forgive Too Soon,* 42.

Arnold, *Why Forgive?* 79.

Countryman, *Forgiven and Forgiving,* 83.

Arnold, *Why Forgive?* 74.

WEEK 7: SEEKING RECONCILIATION

Meninger, *The Process of Forgiveness,* 31.

Countryman, *Forgiven and Forgiving,* 75.

Arnold, *Why Forgive?* 130.

Wuellner, *Forgiveness,* 66.

Arnold, *Why Forgive?* 158.

Lewis B. Smedes, *Forgive and Forget: Healing the Hurts We Don't Deserve* (San Francisco: HarperSanFrancisco, 1984), 181.

WEEK 8: BECOMING THE BELOVED COMMUNITY

Doris Donnelly, "Ambassadors of Reconciliation," *Weavings* 5, no. 1 (January/February 1990): 27.

John S. Mogabgab, "Editor's Introduction," *Weavings* 7, no. 2 (March/April 1992): 2.

Naim Ateek, quoted in Arnold, *Why Forgive?* 38–39.

Alan Paton, quoted in Arnold, *Why Forgive?* frontispiece.

Desmond Mpilo Tutu, *No Future without Forgiveness* (New York: Doubleday, 1999), 282.

Countryman, *Forgiven and Forgiving,* 115.

COMPANION SONG
Piano Accompaniment Score

Lyrics by Marjorie Thompson

Music by Dean McIntyre

Optional cut for short version: omit measures 19-34.

Copyright 2000, Upper Room Books.

pan - ions on the jour - ney, com - pan - ions

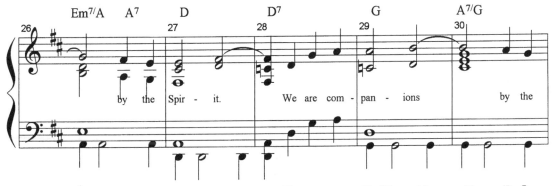

by the Spir - it. We are com - pan - ions by the

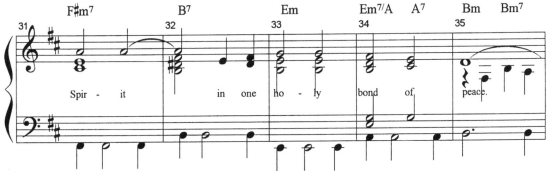

Spir - it in one ho - ly bond of peace.

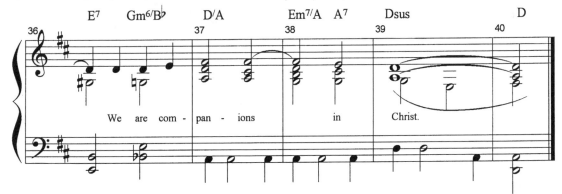

We are com - pan - ions in Christ.

Explanation of the Peace, Hope, and Justice Prayer Candle

The Peace, Hope, and Justice prayer candle celebrates the truth that the light of Christ shines through the darkness, pain, and violence in the world, symbolized by the barbed wire that surrounds the candle. Individuals and groups are invited to light the candle daily (or regularly), while at the same time taking a moment to pray for a particular situation of struggle and pain in the world.

The original prayer candle served as an important symbol of resistance against apartheid in South Africa. It was lit during services of worship while the names of those in government detention were read aloud and prayed for. To this day the prayer candle remains a powerful symbol of protest against injustice and suffering in the world.

This particular candle is handcrafted by unemployed people living in Ivory Park, an impoverished informal settlement area in South Africa near Johannesburg where Upper Room Ministries has an outreach center. For most of the craftspeople, this is their only source of income. All net proceeds from the sale of this candle benefit those craftspeople through the Nehemiah Project, an economic empowerment project created by two Methodist churches in South Africa. Note that the craftsperson who made your candle has signed it on the bottom.

By purchasing this candle, you and your group are already lighting a candle in the midst of darkness in one corner of the world.

Hobson United Methodist Church offers these candles in support of South Africa. To order, make a $20.00 contribution payable to "Hobson UMC." Mailing address is Hobson UMC, c/o Janet Wolf, 1512 Cedar Lane, Nashville, TN 37212 (USA).

About the Author

Marjorie J. Thompson is perhaps best known as the author of *Soul Feast*, a book on Christian spiritual practice that is widely used both in congregations and seminaries. She has also written a book on the spiritual nurture of children in the home entitled *Family: The Forming Center* (Upper Room Books, 1996). Her articles have appeared in *Weavings*, *Worship*, *The Upper Room Disciplines*, and other publications.

In 1996 Marjorie became Director of the Pathways Center for Spiritual Leadership, a program position with Upper Room Ministries. She played a central role in the development of the core resource, *Companions in Christ*, and continues as Spiritual Director to the program.

Marjorie is an ordained minister in the Presbyterian Church, USA. She holds degrees from Swarthmore College and McCormick Theological Seminary. Prior to ordination she was a Research Fellow at Yale Divinity School where she was mentored by Henri Nouwen. Marjorie and her husband, John Mogabgab, live near Nashville, Tennessee.